Interpreting the Tokyo War Crimes Trial:
A Sociopolitical Analysis

INTERPRETING THE TOKYO WAR CRIMES TRIAL:
A Sociopolitical Analysis

Kayoko Takeda

THE UNIVERSITY OF OTTAWA PRESS

OTTAWA 2010

The University of Ottawa Press acknowledges with gratitude the support extended to its publishing list by Heritage Canada through its Book Publishing Industry Development Program, by the Canada Council for the Arts, by the Canadian Federation for the Humanities and Social Sciences through its Aid to Scholarly Publications Program, by the Social Sciences and Humanities Research Council, and by the University of Ottawa.

We also gratefully acknowledge The Monterey Institute of International Studies whose financial support has contributed to the publication of this book.

www.press.uottawa.ca

Library and Archives Canada Cataloguing in Publication

Takeda, Kayoko
    Interpreting the Tokyo War Crimes Tribunal : a sociopolitical analysis / Kayoko Takeda.

Translation of: Tōkyō Saiban ni okeru tsūyaku.
Includes bibliographical references and index.
ISBN 978-0-7766-0729-0

    1. Tokyo Trial, Tokyo, Japan, 1946-1948. 2. Court interpreting and translating--Japan. 3. International Military Tribunal for the Far East. 4. War crime trials--Japan. I. Title.

KZ1181.T34 2010   341.6'90268   C2010-903973-4

TABLE OF CONTENTS

Acknowledgements

This book has been made possible by the assistance and support of many people. First and foremost, my deepest gratitude goes to those who kindly and patiently responded in person, by e-mail and on the telephone to my inquiries about the experiences of the linguists who worked at the Tokyo Trial. They are Takashi Oka, Yukio Kawamoto, Grant Ichikawa, Sueo Ito, George Moore, Yuri Furuno, Ken Shimanouchi, Makoto Kawakami, Michi Itami, Naomi Itami, Sarah Zimmerman, Yasuko Masaki and Masukazu Kusayanagi. Their contributions undoubtedly enhanced the people-focused approach of the book.

This work originates from the doctoral dissertation I submitted to the Universitat Rovira i Virgili in Tarragona, Spain. I was fortunate enough to be advised by the best team of professors that any interpreting researcher could hope for. I would like to extend my heartfelt thanks to my co-supervisors, Franz Pöchhacker and Miriam Shlesinger; the director of the doctoral programme, Anthony Pym; and the other members of the defense committee, Daniel Gile, Ingrid Kurz, Minako O'Hagan and Jordi Mas López. Their constructive criticism shaped my subsequent work and led to the writing of this book.

In addition, I would like to thank the following people who read my dissertation, its derivatives, and the manuscript of this book, in part or in whole, and provided valuable input: Joe Harvin, Koko Peters, Hideko Russell, Yuma Totani, Kaede Johnson, John Olmsted, Mike Hawkey and Masaomi Kondo. Many thanks are also due to Tomie Watanabe, who kindly provided important materials, and to my former students at the Monterey Institute of International Studies, who assisted me in many ways during the research.

I am indebted, for their generous support of my research activities, to the Mark and Lundeen Funds of the Monterey Institute, the Japan Foundation, the Matsushita International Foundation, and the Center for International Studies at Rikkyo University in Tokyo. I am especially grateful to Dean Renee Jourdenais of the Graduate School of Translation, Interpretation, and Language Education at the Monterey Institute for her timely support for this particular project.

Last, but not least, my deep appreciation goes to Luise von Flotow, the series editor, and the editors, Eric Nelson, Marie Clausén and Patrick Heenan at the University of Ottawa Press. Because of their support and guidance, many of the linguists at the Tokyo Trial now have voices again. I thank them for believing in this project, and I salute their continuing contributions to the growing field of Translation and Interpreting Studies through their work in the Perspective on Translation series.

Earlier versions of portions of Chapters 4, 5, and 6, and of the Conclusion, appeared in *FORUM* 5:1, *Interpreting* 10:1, *Across Languages and Cultures* 10:1, and *META* 54:2. A version of this book specifically oriented to a Japanese readership was published as *Tokyo saiban ni okeru tsuyaku* by Misuzu Shobo in 2008.

Introduction

"Impartiality and avoidance of conflict of interest" is a canon universally found in codes of ethics for court interpreters today. Some codes provide a list of circumstances that potentially create perceived or real conflicts of interest for interpreters, as when, for example, the interpreter is a friend, associate or relative of a party to the proceedings, counsel for a party, or a witness involved in the proceedings, or has previously been employed by one of the parties (see, for example, Hewitt 1995; Massachusetts 1988; Wisconsin 2002). Whether it be a case against a drug dealer, a terrorist or a pirate who needs an interpreter's services, it seems hardly conceivable for a court to hire an interpreter who was a subordinate of the defendant or a member of the group to which the suspect belonged, unless, that is, it could not find any other interpreter of the language that the defendant speaks.

This highly unusual situation is exactly what happened in Tokyo, right after the Second World War, at the International Military Tribunal for the Far East (IMTFE). The proceedings of the IMTFE, more commonly known as the Tokyo War Crimes Tribunal or the Tokyo Trial, essentially amounted to the Japanese counterpart of the Nuremberg Trial. Here, in the court proceedings against Japanese war crimes suspects, the communication across different languages was mediated by Japanese government employees and other Japanese nationals.

Of the handful who interpreted the proceedings, about half were associated with the Japanese Ministry of Foreign Affairs and the rest were Japanese citizens with bilingual backgrounds, including two former soldiers of the Japanese Imperial Army. One of the interpreters was the son of a war crimes suspect who testified for the defense during the trial. Given the fact that three former foreign ministers, two high-ranking diplomats and seventeen military leaders were included among the twenty-eight defendants, these interpreters were, in effect, working in a trial in which the lives of their former superiors were at stake.

Further complicating this unusual arrangement were four *Nisei* (second-generation Japanese Americans) who monitored the Japanese interpreters' work throughout the trial and, if it appeared necessary, corrected it. They were all *Kibei* (*Nisei* who had had some schooling in Japan and had then returned to the United States). Because of their experience and education in Japan, *Kibei* had been most readily suspected of disloyalty to the United States and had suffered prejudice, even from other Japanese Americans, before the end of the war. In fact, with the exception of one of them, who was teaching at the U.S. Navy's elite Japanese language school, all these monitors had been detained in an internment camp as "enemy aliens" after Japan's attack on Pearl Harbor, and had been recruited directly from the camp by the U.S. Army to work in military intelligence against Japan during the Pacific War. With this extraordinary background, these *Kibei* linguists arrived at the IMTFE to work as monitors of the Japanese interpreters' work. (The term 'linguists' is used in this book to refer to all those who worked in language-related functions during the war and the trial, since that is how they were referred to in the relevant documents.) For these monitors, the accused were leaders of their parents' homeland, people who shared their cultural heritage and, perhaps, people whom they may have admired during their schooling in Japan.

On top of this complex arrangement, two U.S. military officers were involved in the interpreting and translation services during the Tokyo Trial. (Both are referred to in the relevant archival documents as "Caucasians," which is now a somewhat outdated term but is retained in this book for convenience.) When there was any dispute over interpretations or translations, it was referred to the Language Arbitration Board, which consisted of one member appointed by the Tribunal, one representing the defense and one representing the prosecution. The one appointed by the Tribunal was designated the "language arbiter," a role performed by two Caucasian officers at different times over the course of the trial. Although the first arbiter had been born and raised in Japan and was fluent in Japanese, the other had limited Japanese proficiency. Whether proficient in Japanese or not, the arbiter, who was seated on the prosecution's side of the courtroom, was responsible for ruling on translation and interpreting disputes, and came to the lectern to announce the board's ruling whenever the occasion arose.

Why did the Tribunal establish this three-tier structure for its interpreting system? Why did three ethnically and socially different groups of people engage in different functions within the interpreting process? Why were citizens of the defeated nation hired to work in proceedings against their former superiors? Were all the linguists competent? How did the Japanese interpreters and *Nisei* monitors behave during the proceedings against former leaders of Japan? These are the main questions addressed in this book.

Research

Notwithstanding the uniqueness of the interpreting arrangements at the IMTFE and the historical significance of the trial itself as the Japanese counterpart of the Nuremberg Trial, there has been very little research on the interpreting at the Tokyo Trial. The sole exception is Tomie Watanabe's MA thesis (1998), which is written in Japanese. Watanabe mainly relied on the transcripts of the trial and several books written by historians and participants to present a general description of the interpreting arrangements and to analyze the interpreting errors and "interventions" by monitors and interpreters during the testimony of the former War Minister and Prime Minister Hideki Tojo. The thesis is a significant work, being the first academic inquiry into interpreting at the Tokyo Trial, but it does not pay much attention to contextual factors, nor does it address fundamental questions such as why the hierarchical structure was created and how the behaviour of the linguists could be related to their respective positions within this hierarchy.

In attempting to answer these questions, I have paid close attention to the historical and political context of the trial, as well as to the social and cultural backgrounds of the linguists. In addition to the two sets of trial transcripts, one in English and the other in Japanese, many other sources have been consulted, including interviews with two surviving Japanese interpreters, *Nisei* translators, and the families of some of the linguists who worked at the trial; relevant tribunal documents, films, and photographs; archival documents of the U.S. operations in occupied Japan and the activities of the Japanese Ministry of Foreign Affairs; literature concerning the U.S. military language programmes and wartime intelligence activities, and Japanese war crimes in general; and newspaper articles from post-war Japan. The archival documents, including some that have only recently been declassified, as well as the films and photographs, were obtained primarily from the U.S. National Archives at College Park, Maryland, the MacArthur Memorial Library & Archives in Norfolk, Virginia, the Japanese American Veterans Association, the Archives at the University of Colorado at Boulder, and, in Tokyo, the National Diet Library, the Diplomatic Record Office of the Ministry of Foreign Affairs, and the National Archives of Japan.

A People-Focused and Contextualized Approach

Through the examination of these materials, this book aims to describe the interpreting arrangements at the Tokyo Trial in detail, and to analyze the interpreting phenomena it exhibited in sociopolitical terms such as power, control, trust, race, politics and negotiation. The focus is decidedly placed on people, not texts. In other words, this book looks into where these linguists were situated in historical, political, social and cultural contexts, rather than limiting the object of analysis to microlinguistic or discursive aspects of interpreting reflected in the transcripts. This approach follows Anthony Pym's argument (1998a, x) that people (translators), not texts (translations), are the key to understanding why a given translation was produced at a certain place in a certain time in history. As Pym discusses elsewhere (2006, 15), a mediator-centred approach necessarily leads to the consideration of the social context in which translators and interpreters operate.

It is with this people-focused approach, incorporating broader contextualization, that this book explores why the three-tier interpreting arrangement was devised and explains the complex standing of the *Nisei* linguists, who had to use their language and cultural skills against people of shared cultural heritage during and after the war. The book also analyzes how the interpreting procedures were formed during the trial proceedings, focusing on the socialization of untrained interpreters and the interactive aspect of the development of the interpreting procedures. Further, it will examine the behaviour of some of the interpreters and monitors, and of the language arbiter, looking into their relative positions in the power constellations of the trial and in the hierarchy of language competence.

Structure

Although the Tokyo Trial has never ceased to attract attention from historians, political scientists, the media and activists in Japan, it does not seem to attract the same level of interest outside the country. While there have been more than a hundred Japanese books that exclusively treat the Tokyo Trial, only a dozen can be found in the English language. This book, therefore, starts in Chapter 1 with a brief introduction to the IMTFE, including its historical background, and the key facts and controversies surrounding it.

Chapter 2 provides a detailed description of the interpreting arrangements at the trial, including the languages used, the recruitment of the interpreters and translators, the interpreting equipment and booth, the mechanism for correcting errors, translation problems, and the effect of interpreting on the proceedings.

Chapter 3 presents profiles of the main linguists who worked at the IMTFE, drawing on interviews and archival documents. The descriptions of their family and educational backgrounds should shed some light on the historical, political, social and cultural contexts that brought them to the Tokyo Trial.

Chapter 4 provides detailed analysis of three distinct features of interpreting at the Tokyo Trial: the hierarchy of the linguists, the complex nature of the standing of the *Nisei* monitors as "in between" and the process of trial and error through which the Tribunal established its interpreting procedures during the initial stages of the trial.

The behaviour of some of the interpreters and monitors is discussed in Chapter 5, which focuses on the testimony of Hideki Tojo, who was considered the main "face" of the trial. The nature of the monitors' interjections, and the interactions among the court participants, interpreters, monitors and the language arbiter during the proceedings are examined with particular attention to the relative positions of the different linguists in the explicit hierarchy of the Language Section, as well as in the implicit hierarchy created by their varying language competences.

The key findings discussed in Chapters 4 and 5 are revisited for a sociopolitical analysis in Chapter 6. Issues of trust, power and control are discussed in order to explain the three-tier structure of the interpreting system and the behaviour of some of the linguists, and the ambivalent position of the *Nisei* is examined using the notions of "autonomous" and "heteronomous" interpreters (see Cronin 2002, 2006). The concept of negotiation of norms is applied in analyzing the formation of the interpreting procedures during the trial proceedings.

The Conclusion elucidates the significance of the interpreting at the Tokyo Trial in two historical contexts. One concerns its position in the history of conference interpreting in Japan, and the other draws parallels between the experiences of the *Nisei* monitors and the situations of some of the linguists currently serving in conflict zones in which the United States is involved. Finally, the overall argument of this book will be reiterated: interpreting at the Tokyo War Crimes Tribunal is a case in point for the call for broader contextualization, beyond microlinguistic analysis, in order to achieve a fuller understanding of interpreting phenomena.

For the Linguists

Interpreting at the Nuremberg Tribunal has been cited as the origin of simultaneous interpreting, or, more accurately, "the coming of age" (Baigorri 1999, 34) of simultaneous interpreting, or "the first time that simultaneous interpretation was used consistently and for extended periods of time" (Moser-Mercer 2005, 208). The Nuremberg proceedings have therefore attracted attention from both scholars and practising interpreters. While Francesca Gaiba (1998) has presented the most extensive scholarly work on the topic to date, people who actually served as interpreters at Nuremberg have also written articles and books about their experiences (see, for example, Gesse 2005, Sonnenfeldt 2006).

In contrast, the proceedings in Tokyo have become an all but forgotten chapter in the history of interpreting. Unlike the Nuremberg interpreters, almost none of the interpreters or monitors who worked at the Tokyo Trial became professional interpreters. While some of the Nuremberg interpreters continued working as conference interpreters at the United Nations and in other international settings, the Japanese interpreters and the *Nisei* monitors alike returned to their "real" jobs or followed different career paths after the trial. No longer interpreting, these linguists had neither reason nor opportunity to discuss their experiences at the trial publicly in the interpreting community. Further, given the negative sentiment toward the Tokyo Trial among those Japanese who denounced it as "victors' justice," and the possible stigma attached to having been part of the team that facilitated communication at this controversial trial, it is understandable that the interpreters did not actively seek opportunities to discuss their experiences. Hence, their stories were buried in history for more than fifty years.

The interpreters, monitors and language arbiters had all undergone hardships and challenges in different forms during the fierce and cruel war between Japan and the United States. They were then called upon to take up an unprecedented task of historical importance and tremendous difficulty: interpreting for the international court proceedings trying Japanese war criminals. This book is dedicated to all the people who tackled this extremely challenging assignment with such courage, self-sacrifice and professional determination.

Note on Japanese Terms and Names

For ease of reading, terms from Japanese are cited in this book without any accents to indicate vowel length. In addition, except in the list of References at the end of the book, names of Japanese persons are given in the Western style, with personal name first and family name second (for example, Hideki Tojo), rather than in the Japanese style with family name first (Tojo Hideki).

CHAPTER 1

THE TRIAL

Toward the end of the Second World War, the leaders of three Allied nations—the United States, the United Kingdom and China—met on July 26, 1945, and issued the Potsdam Declaration on the Japanese surrender. This document included a reference to the "stern justice" that was to "be meted out to all war criminals, including those who have visited cruelties upon prisoners." Following the atomic bombings of Hiroshima on August 6 and of Nagasaki on August 9, Emperor Hirohito's announcement of surrender was broadcast to his subjects on August 15. The official ending of hostilities was marked when the Instrument of Surrender was signed by representatives of the Japanese government on board the USS *Missouri* in Tokyo Bay on September 2, 1945.

The prosecution of war criminals had been discussed among the Allied nations in the early 1940s, and the United Nations War Crimes Commission had been established in October 1943 to start gathering evidence of war crimes. Based on its investigations, the Special Far Eastern and Pacific Committee of the War Crimes Commission recommended on August 25, 1945, that Japanese war criminals be "surrendered to or apprehended by the United Nations for trial before an international military tribunal," and, as Supreme Commander of the Allied Powers (SCAP), U.S. Army General Douglas MacArthur was given the authority to prepare for the establishment and operation of the Tribunal.

The occupation of Japan by the Allied Powers started on August 28. MacArthur arrived in Japan as SCAP on August 30, and one of the first operations he directed was the arrest and prosecution of Japanese war criminals. On September 11, MacArthur ordered the arrest of thirty-nine individuals suspected of having committed war crimes, including the former Prime Minister and War Minister General Hideki Tojo. More arrests followed. Within a few months, more than one hundred war crimes suspects were being detained in Sugamo Prison in Tokyo. Although the charter for the Nuremberg Trials had already been announced on August 8, it took months for the Tokyo counterpart to be established. Meanwhile, President Harry S. Truman appointed Joseph Keenan, former head of the U.S. Justice Department's criminal division, to serve as chief prosecutor for the trial of Japanese war criminals. Keenan arrived in Japan on December 6 with a team of nearly forty lawyers and aides. Unlike at Nuremberg, where the United States, the United Kingdom, France and the Soviet Union each had its own prosecution team, there was a single prosecution team for Tokyo, led by Keenan and comprising representatives from eleven Allied nations. The International Prosecution Section was established on December 8, the fourth anniversary of the attack on Pearl Harbor according to the Japanese calendar, within the offices of the occupation headquarters (itself known as SCAP by this point). It was not until January 19, 1946, however, that the jurisdiction, functions and procedural guidelines of the Tribunal were announced, in the form of the Charter of the International Military Tribunal for the Far East, commonly known as the Tokyo Charter. This charter had been drafted by the U.S. prosecution team, following the model of the Nuremberg Charter, and was approved and announced by MacArthur. It was later amended following consultations with the other Allied nations.

With the charter in place, each of the nine signatories to the Japanese Instrument of Surrender nominated a judge, and MacArthur officially appointed these judges on February 15, 1946. They were from Australia, Canada, the Republic of China, France, the Netherlands, New Zealand, the Soviet Union, the United Kingdom and the United States. The Australian judge, Sir William Webb, was appointed President of the Tribunal, despite concerns that he had been the chief investigator of the Japanese army's atrocities against Australian prisoners of war and might be regarded as biased against the Japanese defendants. He remained President of the Tribunal throughout the trial. Prompted by a call from the Far Eastern Commission, the Allied Powers' highest policy-making agency for the occupation of Japan, for further representations on the bench, MacArthur amended the Tribunal's charter on April 26 to add judges from India and the Philippines, making a total of eleven judges.

As the International Prosecution Section interrogated "Class A" war crimes suspects in Sugamo Prison, Japanese lawyers were retained to represent them. Concerned about these lawyers' unfamiliarity with the Anglo-American law of the Tribunal, on February 14 the Japanese government requested that MacArthur provide British and American lawyers for the defense. Since British lawyers were not permitted by British law to practise under a foreign jurisdiction, arrangements were made to bring fifteen lawyers from the United States. Despite urgent requests, however, they did not arrive in Tokyo until May 17, two weeks after the opening of the trial.

The Proceedings

On April 29, 1946, the indictment was formally lodged with the Tribunal against twenty-eight "Class A" defendants, all of whom had been military and political leaders in wartime Japan. They were accused of "crimes against peace (Class A)," "conventional war crimes (Class B)" and "crimes against humanity (Class C)." Despite some reservations in certain countries, such as Australia, about the decision to protect Emperor Hirohito from prosecution, the Allied governments ultimately agreed not to proceed with his trial for the sake of avoiding the possibility of disruption to their larger goal of constructing a democratic Japan. For various reasons, which are still being debated by historians, the Allies also failed to bring to justice some of those who had committed serious war crimes, such as biological and chemical warfare, experiments on Chinese and Russian prisoners of war and civilians and forced prostitution of Korean women (see Dower 1999, 465; Bix 2000, 617; Drea 2006, 4–7; Awaya 2006, 81–114).

The Tribunal convened on May 3, 1946, with the statement by Sir William Webb, often quoted since, that "there has been no more important criminal trial in all history." The case for the prosecution started right away and lasted until January 24, 1947. The case for the defense followed and lasted until January 12, 1948. Rebuttals and summations by both sides were concluded on April 4, and the Tribunal adjourned until November 4, when the delivery of the judgment began. With the completion of sentencing, the Tribunal adjourned on November 12, 1948. The length of the trial in Tokyo is often cited as one of the major differences from the Nuremberg Trials, the first of which was concluded in less than one year. According to Greg Bradsher (n. d., 180–81), the language difficulty is generally believed to have been the major cause of the relatively extreme length of the proceedings, but there were other factors prolonging them, such as the complexity of the subject matter and the absence of relevant official records, since the Japanese Army had destroyed many documents around the end of the war. A total of 419 witnesses testified in 818 sessions over 417 days, and 779 affidavits and depositions were presented. Admitted exhibits in the form of documents totalled around 30,000 pages, and the English transcripts of the court proceedings, excluding exhibits and the judgment, number 48,488 pages.

During the trial two of the defendants died of natural causes and one had a mental breakdown and was found incompetent to stand trial. The remaining twenty-five were all found guilty by a majority vote of the judges, although separate dissenting opinions were submitted by the judges from the Philippines, France, the Netherlands and India, as well as by Webb. Seven of the defendants, including Hideki Tojo, were sentenced to death by hanging, sixteen to life imprisonment and two to lesser terms. The executions took place inside Sugamo Prison on December 23, 1948 (which happened to be the birthday of Emperor Hirohito's son, the current Emperor Akihito, and is now a national holiday). Four of the imprisoned died while serving their sentences, but the Japanese government paroled the rest in 1956 and released them unconditionally in 1958.

Controversies

The Tokyo Trial has been viewed in both positive and negative lights. Some refer approvingly to the role it played in exposing some of the Japanese military's atrocities in China and other Asian countries, both to the world in general and, in particular, to the citizens of Japan, who had been kept in the dark about some of their leaders' and soldiers' wartime activities. (Takashi Oka, who was one of the interpreters at the trial, pointed this out to this author when interviewed in Washington, DC, on December 11, 2005.) Some even see this as the starting point for Japan's confrontation with its wartime record and as an important precursor for later developments of international criminal justice (see Totani 2008).

As for criticism, there is plenty. First and foremost, the Tokyo Trial has been criticized by historians, ideologues and participants in the proceedings as "victors' justice," an exercise in revenge or a U.S.-led theatrical "show" trial marred by political whims (see, for example, Pal 1953; Minear 1971; Röling and Cassese 1993; Dower 1999). Some of these critics also emphasize the selectiveness of the prosecutions, which, as has been mentioned, exempted the Emperor and many war criminals, and the forced application of the categorization of war crimes at Nuremberg to what they argue was a different situation in Japan.

The legitimacy of the IMTFE has remained a controversial issue in Japan even sixty years after the conclusion of the trial, and has become one of the major themes of nationalist and revisionist views on Japan's wartime actions. The standard argument is that the Tokyo Trial was biased, unfair and one-sided, especially in its failure to address the actions of the Allied powers, such as the atomic bombings, and that it was based on the retroactive application of laws that had not existed at the time the war crimes in question were committed. Discussion of the IMTFE and its long-lasting effects on Japan, under the general rubric of *Tokyo Saiban shikan* ("Tokyo Trial view of history"), have gained momentum every time a Japanese Prime Minister has visited Yasukuni Shrine in Tokyo, where "Class A" war criminals are enshrined among other war dead, as well as every time disputes have arisen with China and South Korea over the publication in Japan of controversial history textbooks with revisionist views.

The validity of the Tokyo War Crimes Tribunal does not fall within the direct scope of this book, but the political nature of the trial must be taken into full consideration nonetheless. The facts that the Tokyo Trial was carried out by the victor nations against the vanquished and that its operation was essentially led by the U.S. military authorities are deeply connected with the selection of linguists, the arrangements for interpreting mechanisms and the development of the actual interpreting procedures. Based on an awareness of this political context, Chapter 2 examines the who, what, where, when, why and how of interpreting at the Tokyo Trial.

CHAPTER 2

THE INTERPRETING ARRANGEMENTS

The aim of this chapter is to describe the overall interpreting arrangements at the Tokyo Trial in detail, including the languages used, how the court handled "non-official" languages, how the linguists were recruited and assigned, their compensation, their equipment, the modes of interpreting they engaged in, the challenges they faced in the actual task of interpreting, and the system used for correcting interpreting errors. It also discusses the work done by the translators in order to provide a fuller picture of how the Tribunal addressed its language needs, both oral and written. Finally, some comments by historians are introduced regarding the effect of interpreting on the trial proceedings.

The Official Languages of the Tribunal

The use of interpreting and translation at the Tokyo Trial was provided for in the Tokyo Charter (of which the official text is available in Pritchard 1998 among others). Under the heading "Fair Trial for Accused," Article 9 (b) of the Charter states:

> Language. The trial and related proceedings shall be conducted in English and in the language of the accused. Translations of documents and other papers shall be provided as needed and requested.

Accordingly, interpretation between English and Japanese in the consecutive mode (as discussed below) was offered throughout the trial, but Russian simultaneous interpretation was also available as a Soviet-operated stand-alone arrangement for the Soviet judge, who understood neither English nor Japanese. "As a courtesy" (according to Brackman 1987, 213–14), one of the three channels of the interpreting equipment was assigned to interpretation into Russian.

Handling of Non-Official Languages

During the trial the Tribunal also used interpreters of Chinese, French, Dutch, German, Russian and Mongolian when witnesses or prosecutors spoke in these languages. However, the transcripts of the proceedings (see *Kyokuto kokusai gunji saiban sokkiroku* and Pritchard 1998) indicate that the Tribunal had not anticipated or prepared for the use of languages other than English and Japanese. During the early stages of the trial a significant amount of time was spent, inside and outside the courtroom, discussing how testimony in languages other than English and Japanese should be handled and whether the use of "non-official" languages by prosecutors should be permitted in court at all.

When the first Chinese-speaking witness, General Ching The-Chun of the Republic of China, appeared before the Tribunal on July 22, 1946, the initial arrangement was to provide relay interpreting with Japanese as the pivot language between Chinese and English. In other words, Chinese or English was consecutively interpreted into Japanese, then the Japanese interpretation was consecutively interpreted into English or Chinese. This system was devised because the Language Section, which managed the work of all the linguists for the Tribunal, could not find an interpreter who could work directly between Chinese and English. Although a Chinese member of the prosecution had been considered as a potential interpreter between Chinese and English, concerns about the propriety of having him interpret for a witness produced by the prosecution prevented him from assuming the role. However, U.S. counsel became frustrated because they had to hear two unfamiliar languages (Chinese, then Japanese) before the English interpretation was delivered, and voiced their concern that this "double translation" might be "very imperfect" (IMTFE Transcripts, pp. 2300–2301). The President of the Tribunal, who had not previously been informed of this issue, handed down a ruling on the spot, accepting the prosecution's suggestion that the Tribunal use W. F. S. Fang, an English-speaking secretary to Mei Ju-ao, the judge from the Republic of China, as an interpreter between Chinese and English. Subsequently, English became the pivot language in relay interpreting between the three languages: Chinese or Japanese was first interpreted into English consecutively, and then the English interpretation was interpreted into Japanese or Chinese. Fang interpreted throughout the morning of July 23, 1946, but after that a few other Chinese personnel took over his role. However, the poor performance of these ad hoc interpreters drew questions from both the defense and the prosecution as to the accuracy of the interpretation, which frequently disrupted the court proceedings. Finally, during the testimony of Henry Pu-Yi, the former Emperor of Manchukuo, who appeared as a witness for the prosecution from August 16 to August 27, 1946, the President of the Tribunal personally appealed to General MacArthur by letter (now in the MacArthur Memorial Library & Archives) to enlist the aid of the occupation authorities in finding competent Chinese interpreters. In response, MacArthur sent his own interpreter to the court on August 26, and made an arrangement to bring more interpreters in from Shanghai.

Having these ad hoc interpreters for the pivot language presented a challenge to the Japanese interpreters as well. According to Takashi Oka, one of the Japanese interpreters who worked regularly throughout the trial (interviewed by the author in Washington, DC, on December 11, 2005), the most difficult task he faced during the proceedings was to relay the Chinese interpreter's unclear Chinese-to-English interpretation into Japanese (as well as to relay the Dutch-to-English interpretation into Japanese). The problems with this relay arrangement are probably what prompted the IMTFE to ask the counterpart Tribunal in Nuremberg about its system of handling multiple languages at the same time. A telegram from the Secretariat of the IMTFE to its counterpart in Nuremberg, dated August 23, 1946 (and now in U.S. National Archives, Record Group 331), made the following inquiries:

1. How many languages are spoken in the court?

2. How many language translations are spoken simultaneously over the translator device?

3. What is the total number of interpreters and monitors used at any one time?

4. Are the interpreters in the open court or behind glass walls?

5. What is the distance between witness box and interpreters?

6. [Is] More than one court reporter for each language needed by the interpreter?

7. Where are official court reporters seated, near witness or near interpreters?

8. How much space is used by interpretation personnel involving interpreters, monitors and others?

9. How are counsel, witness and interpreters' speech activities coordinated?

Coming almost four months after the start of the trial, this belated inquiry indicates that the Tribunal had not fully prepared for the use of a third language in court. The response from Nuremberg, dated August 27, 1946 (and also in Record Group 331), gives clear answers to all nine of the questions:

1. Number of languages spoken in courtroom—four. (By use of special arrangement any fifth language may also be used.).

2. Three language translations are spoken simultaneously over the equipment. That is, speaker uses one court language, interpreters interpret into other three.

3. Total number of interpreters in use at one time—twelve, with one monitor.

4. Interpreters are in open court behind unroffed [presumably a typo for "unroofed"] glass partitions.

5. Distance between witness box and interpreters—fifteen feet, but distance is immaterial as both are mutually connected by microphones, earphones, and wires.

6. Number of court reporters for each language depends on proficiency of individual reporter. For safety, we have been using two reporters for each language at any one time. Total of about nine reporters for each language to provide coverage for a six-hour working day.

7. Official court reporters are seated between witness stand, prosecution, and defense speaking position. They are also between

the bench and the dock, at approximately the center of the courtroom. Again position not important as are connected with wires and earphones to both speaker and interpreters.

8. Space needed by interpreter personnel—two tables, six interpreters at each, with comfortable movie [theatre] type seats. Space approximately six by fifteen feet. Monitor sits at one end of interpreter tables. In addition, two positions necessary for technical personnel, one in the courtroom before console three by ten feet to maintain constant volume level on various microphones. Other can be located outside courtroom but should be able to see into courtroom to maintain general check on amplifiers and system as a whole.

9. Speech activities coordinated as follows: Prosecution and defense speak from single table with microphone. They address the court in turn. Earphones provided at table. Judges have individual microphones and earphones, and recognize speakers as they wish. Witness stand also has a microphone and earphones. In questioning witness, the prosecution or defense uses own language, which is interpreted simultaneously into witnesses [*sic*] language so that he understands as soon as question is completed. Witness then answers in own language, which in turn is simultaneously interpreted into prosecutor's or defense's language. There is no delay between question and answer. Wish to emphasize that interpretation is simultaneous, that interpretation into all three language[s] begins as the speaker begins speaking [and] is finished within a few seconds of the time the speaker is finished. Requires highly skilled and highly trained personnel. Interpreters responsible for knowing the language of the speaker, so if Russian prosecutor approaches speaking stand, three interpreters who interpret respectively Russian into English, Russian into French, and Russian into German, are ready and waiting to start interpreting as soon as Russian prosecutor begins speaking. Interpreters listen and interpret at the same time.

This correspondence indicates that the court in Nuremberg, going into the ninth month of its proceedings, had a well-established interpreting system in place, based on a good understanding of the interpreters' competence requirements. However, this instructive information cannot have been very useful for the Tokyo Tribunal, because of the absence of simultaneous interpreting (as discussed below).

When the French prosecutor Robert L. Oneto opened his case in French on September 30, 1946, the defense raised an objection, citing non-compliance with the Tokyo Charter, which stipulated English and the language of the accused as the languages to be used to conduct the proceedings. The defense also complained about the difficulty of monitoring the accuracy of interpretation, since there were very few who understood French, and the delay and inconvenience caused by Oneto's refusal to speak English. Chief Prosecutor Joseph Keenan argued that the Charter did not exclude languages other than English and Japanese, and that the English and Japanese translations of Oneto's statement had been provided to the interpreters. After some discussion, the President of the Tribunal overruled the defense's objection and allowed Oneto to speak in French. Later in the proceedings, however, Oneto referred to certain documents that had not been translated into French beforehand. He read these materials aloud in the original English, and made some extemporaneous remarks in English as well, although, because of his accent, the interpreters and the court reporter could not understand him. Sir William Webb commented in open court (IMTFE Transcripts, p. 6736):

> The prosecution had better reconsider its attitude in this matter. We have done our best to meet the position we have reached. We feel we should not be called upon to waste time when we know that on the French staff there are men who speak English wonderfully well. We have done our best to meet the prosecution. The prosecution must do their best to meet the Bench. The difficulty

is [that] the Bench can follow Mr. Oneto with difficulty; the interpreters cannot follow him, and at least one of his statements has not yet been interpreted.

A long discussion followed. Frustrated, Webb ordered a recess, but even after the recess the discussion on the relay interpreting arrangement continued. Finally, with apparent irritation, Webb made a ruling that only English was to be used throughout the French case. One of the U.S. prosecutors indicated that Oneto wished to comment, but Webb flatly responded, "The interpreters will not understand him, so it is useless for him [Oneto] to talk" (IMTFE Transcripts, p. 6742). He then adjourned the Tribunal.

The next day, after a brief exchange between Webb and Keenan on the use of languages other than English and Japanese, Oneto started speaking in French again, despite the court's ruling. Webb complained, "He is still speaking French. This is almost contempt" (IMTFE Transcripts, p. 6746), and ordered a recess. This incident is described rather dramatically in the newspapers of the time. For example, under the headline "French Prosecutor Stalls Proceedings of Tokyo Tribunal," the *Nippon Times* (an English-language newspaper now called the *Japan Times*) reported on October 2:

President Webb suddenly declared that the court will adjourn and began to rise from his bench, with his colleagues following suit. But instead of cutting short his vociferous flow of French, Prosecutor Oneto gripped the microphone and pleaded, in his same native language, "Monsieur le president! Monsieur le president . . ." President Webb, now standing, remarked that the prosecutor was holding the court in contempt, and withdrew, followed by his colleagues, but not until the justices' benches became entirely vacant did Prosecutor Oneto end his shouting to the effect: "I represent the great nation of France. I demand the right to be heard. If not, I will withdraw from the case."

A long, hard discussion continued that day, requiring three extended recesses. Behind the scenes, Webb seems to have been pressed to accept the argument of the prosecutors. According to Arnold C.

Brackman, who observed the trial as a journalist and witness, the French judge threatened to resign if Webb did not allow the use of French in the proceedings (Brackman 1987, 215–16). There was also pressure from the Soviet delegation to let prosecutors speak in their native languages. During one of the recesses, Webb reportedly learned that the Soviet prosecutor intended to speak in Russian to present his case, following Oneto.

After the last recess, which lasted about an hour, Webb finally accepted the prosecution's argument that the Tokyo Charter did not specify that languages other than English and Japanese should not be used. Toward the end of the day, Webb announced, "The Tribunal by a majority has decided to allow the use of French to the extent indicated or suggested by the learned Chief Prosecutor" (IMTFE Transcripts, p. 6782). Thus ended a debate that had occupied the attention of the Tribunal for two days. At the beginning of the third day of Oneto's case, on October 2, 1946, Webb confirmed that the Charter did not exclude the use of any particular language (IMTFE Transcripts, pp. 6787–6790):

> In the first place, I desire to emphasize the fact that we are this morning to deal not with a nation, not with the French nation, but with an individual who represents that nation. If a British or American or Australian or Netherlands prosecutor behaved before this Court as did Mr. Oneto, he would be dealt with in exactly the same way. No Member of this Tribunal entertains any national prejudice. I am sure the gentleman who represents France on this Tribunal does not think otherwise.

> As Mr. Oneto will be practically in the position of a defendant this morning, we will hear him in his own language, if he desires to speak. He may, if he thinks fit, speak in English. . . .

> One reading the record might draw the conclusion that there was some suggestion of discriminatory treatment by this Court. As we left the bench yesterday Mr. Oneto referred to his "great country" in terms that suggested that he was defending its cause here. I do

not know enough French to be able to say just what he did remark, but one of my colleagues who does speak and understand French says that that was the substance of Mr. Oneto's remark. Both of us may have misunderstood Mr. Oneto. But that is one of the reasons why I stressed the fact that this Court has no prejudice against any nation.

Now we would like to hear Mr. Oneto in English or French in explanation of this position.

In response, Oneto stated, in French, "Mr. President, with the authorization of the Court, I wish to continue to use the French language myself, and I will ask Mr. Tavenner, my distinguished colleague, to read in English the documents on which I wish to base my accusations" (IMTFE Transcripts, p. 6790). Oneto asked a U.S. colleague to read documents in order to spare the interpreters and the court reporter having to hear his heavy accent, and himself took the lectern in French for other proceedings. There was no relay interpreting involved. French-to-English and French-to-Japanese interpreters were available, and French was interpreted consecutively into English and Japanese at the same time.

After the incident with Oneto, there was another dispute provoked by the Soviet prosecution team's insistence upon using Russian. Despite Webb's ruling during Oneto's case, the defense objected once more, complaining that the use of French had already disrupted, delayed and prolonged the proceedings, and that allowing the use of Russian would further hinder the fair and smooth operation of the Tribunal. The defense repeated the argument that this was not consistent with the Tokyo Charter, which stipulated that English and Japanese were to be used to conduct the proceedings. Further, the defense insinuated that political considerations were behind the court's decision to allow the Soviet prosecutor to speak in Russian, and that this had been arranged between the United States and the Soviet Union before the proceedings opened. Webb called this line of argument offensive, claimed that the Charter did not exclude a third language, and made a ruling that the Tribunal would allow the language of any of the countries represented in the proceedings (IMTFE Transcripts, pp. 7087–7088):

> We made it so in the French case. I may state that a majority of the Court thought that the Charter did not or does not exclude a third language. Of that majority, some thought the Court had a discretion in the matter, which was to be exercised having regard to the terms of the Charter, more particularly that provision of the Charter against delays. Others of the majority thought [that] there was a duty to allow the language of any of the Prosecution Section to be used: that is to say, the language of any of the countries represented on this Court. I think it works out this way, that we must be satisfied that there will be no undue delay in presenting the case in Russian, and that the case for Russia, or for the Soviet [Union] I should say, cannot be properly presented in English or Japanese. That is the question of fact facing us this afternoon, and it does not involve any political considerations.

The debate over the use of Russian occupied the whole afternoon session on October 4, 1946, but finally, five months after the beginning of the trial, the issue of what languages would be allowed was clarified. During the Soviet stage of the case for the prosecution, Russian-to-Japanese interpreters were available in addition to Soviet interpreters who worked between English and Russian. There was no relay interpreting involved.

Later in the proceedings, during the testimony of a German-speaking witness, interpreters between German and Japanese, and German and English were provided. Relay interpreting was used for testimony given in Dutch and Mongolian, with English and Russian as the pivot language, respectively.

The Language Section

The Tribunal's Secretariat was responsible for administrative work, such as maintaining records, and supervising the court clerk, the marshal and the court reporters. It was headed by a U.S. Army colonel, and an officer was seconded from the occupation headquarters to act as liaison between the Tribunal and the press, as well as between the prosecution and the defense. Attached to the Secretariat were the Reproduction Center, the Photographic Division and the Language Section.

The Language Section, which had a U.S. military officer, active or retired, as its chief, arranged interpreters and monitors to meet the language requirements of the proceedings. The transcripts indicate that four different officers worked as chief of the Language Section at different times during the trial, but most of the comments by a Language Section chief recorded in the transcripts come from the first chief, Ensign David Hornstein. His three successors did not have a good command of Japanese, so Hornstein was probably the only one of the four who was fairly proficient in the language. According to an article in the leading Japanese newspaper, the *Asahi Shimbun* ("Mizugiwadatsu shori buri," July 15, 1946), Hornstein, then only twenty-one years old, was an effective supervisor of the twenty-four interpreters, monitors and court reporters employed as of July 1946. Originally from Pennsylvania, Hornstein had studied Japanese at the University of Washington in Seattle and at the U.S. Navy's Japanese language school in Boulder, Colorado. The article reports that he was chosen as chief of the Language Section and sent to Tokyo in March 1946 because of his fluent Japanese, as well as his knowledge of Japanese political and economic affairs.

Monitors and Language Arbiters

In recruiting monitors to check the interpreters' performance, and language arbiters to make rulings on translation and interpreting disputes, the Language Section looked for those who had worked in military intelligence as linguists during the war and were now working for the occupation authorities in Japan, whether as military personnel or as civilians. Four *Nisei*—David Akira Itami, Sho Onodera, Lanny

Miyamoto and Hidekazu Hayashi—were selected as monitors from this pool, and Major Lardner Moore and Captain Edward Kraft were appointed as language arbiters at different times. (Their backgrounds are discussed in more detail in Chapter 3.)

The monitors and language arbiters were paid on the U.S. military pay scale, but their designations in the scale and the exact amount of their pay remain unknown. According to his personal journal (in Kajiki High School 1949/1987), Itami was hired by the IMTFE as "CAF (clerical, administrative and fiscal service)-11" on April 12, 1946. One document on the roster of the U.S. Army's civilian linguists (see Bishop 1948) shows that Onodera and Hayashi were also given a CAF-11 pay scale rating as of December 31, 1948. The *Civilian Personnel List* issued by the Army's War Crimes Branch on September 22, 1948 (and now in Records Group 153 in the U.S. National Archives) shows that the minimum yearly salaries for relevant grades were US$6,235.20 for CAF-12 and US$4,479.60 for CAF-9. These figures suggest that the monitors at the Tokyo Trial were probably paid about US$470 a month. Considering that, for example, teachers at the American School in Tokyo received only US$244 a month in 1947 (according to the Tokyo American School Fund Campaign's documents in Records Group 554 of the U.S. National Archives), the monitors seem to have earned very attractive salaries.

Recruitment of Interpreters

The interpreters were mainly recruited through the International Prosecution Section, which already had a pool of translators working for it before the Tokyo Trial began; through the Translator and Interpreter Service of SCAP (the occupation headquarters), which had been moved to Japan from the South Pacific after the end of the war; and through the Central Liaison Office affiliated to the

Japanese Ministry of Foreign Affairs, which had been established by the Japanese government, on the orders of SCAP, even before the Allied occupation of Japan officially began on August 28, 1945.

The Ministry dispatched some of its own employees as interpreters to the Tokyo Tribunal, and the Central Liaison Office also began placing advertisements for interpreters as early as August 26, when one such advertisement appeared in the *Asahi Shimbun*. According to one of the interpreters, Toshiro Shimanouchi (quoted in Komatsu 2003, 74), the recruitment effort was led by Viscount Sei'ichi Motono, a former counsellor in the Japanese Embassy in Paris who was still working in the Ministry of Foreign Affairs. Since the number of people who were proficient in both Japanese and English was limited, and very few had any interpreting experience, the terms and conditions set out in the Ministry's advertisements were relatively undemanding. The following advertisement, for example, was published in the English-language *Nippon Times* on September 2:

Interpreters and Guides Wanted

1. A large number of interpreters and guides is necessary for the convenience of the Allied Forces, which have arrived in Japan.

2. The interpreters and guides must be men of over 18 years old, speaking English, no matter whether they speak it well or not. No other qualifications are necessary. No examination is held.

3. A due amount of allowance is given, considering their positions, occupations and other points. Dormitory facilities are provided on the spot they serve, but they are free to go there from their own home.

4. They are adopted as extra secretaries of the Foreign Office in principle.

5. The places where these interpreters and guides are wanted are Atsugi, Yokosuka and Yokohama.

6. Those who want to be their interpreters and guides are requested to come as quickly as possible to the First Section of the Research Bureau of the Foreign Office, care of the fourth floor of the Education Ministry.

The Foreign Office

SCAP itself also placed similar advertisements in the *Nippon Times* almost daily throughout the first few years of the occupation. The wording and details varied, but the first to refer specifically to a "court" appeared on November 6, 1945:

8th Army Military Government, Tokyo Detachment Labor Office

WANTED—MEN ONLY

50 Court Translators (must be able to translate readily from English to Japanese and Japanese to English)

50 Court Interpreters (must be able to translate [sic] readily from English to Japanese and Japanese to English)

This advertisement does not indicate for which "court" the translators and interpreters would be working, or if there was any requirement pertaining to nationality or other credentials. However, considering the fact that the prosecution team for the IMTFE was not formed until December 8, 1946, this advertisement was probably not meant to be specific to the Tokyo Trial, but rather to secure a pool of translators and interpreters for the anticipated trials of Japanese war criminals. Newspaper advertisements for court interpreters continued to run for the duration of the Tokyo Trial and beyond, presumably for the trials, held in Yokohama, of those accused of "Class B" and "Class C" war crimes.

Testing of candidates for posts as interpreters started a few months before the trial in 1946 (see Shimada 2000, 18; Oka 2005, interview by author). The test consisted of having the candidates interpret in a simulated trial. Some orientation on court procedures was given to those who passed the test, but there was virtually no training in interpreting before they were sent to the courtroom because no one was qualified to train them (Shimada 2000, p. 18). There was no Japanese counterpart of Colonel Léon Dostert, an experienced interpreter from the United States who set up the simultaneous interpreting system at Nuremberg and trained some of its interpreters before the trial (Gaiba 1998, 34–38).

An article in the *Nippon Times* of April 26, 1946 (one week before the trial), reported that the selection of "ten Japanese, all well-versed in English," to be employed for the trial was being conducted by the International Prosecution Section, the Tribunal and the Central Liaison Office, and that so far eight had been selected. Of the eight chosen, four were associated with the Ministry of Foreign Affairs: Viscount Motono, the official who had led the recruitment effort; Jun Tsuchiya, a former First Secretary in the Embassy in Stockholm; Tomio Mori, who had been a Third Secretary stationed in Shanghai; and Toshiro Shimanouchi, a secretary of the Ministry. The other four were Masayoshi Hoshimi, an employee of the American Club; Masahito Iwamoto, a former employee of the U.S. Embassy in Tokyo; Hideo Masutani, a former employee of the Japanese Embassy in Washington, DC; and Takashi Oka, a student at Rikkyo University (also known as St. Paul's University, a private Christian institution in Tokyo).

According to Masakazu Shimada (2000, 18–19), about fifteen people were hired as interpreters at the initial stage of the trial, but many of them left after making only brief attempts at interpreting. The composition of the interpreter team was very fluid for the first three months of the trial, but it subsequently settled down to about ten interpreters. According to Tomie Watanabe (1998, 10–11), the transcripts record a total of twenty-seven interpreters between Japanese and English, but only a handful of them worked regularly throughout the proceedings. Those who worked most frequently were Toshiro Shimanouchi (419 sessions), Masakazu Shimada (323 sessions), Takashi Oka (289 sessions), Tomio Mori (216 sessions), Masahito Iwamoto (170 sessions) and Makoto Taji (160 sessions) (Watanabe 1998, 10–11; these Japanese nationals are profiled in Chapter 3).

Documents issued by the Ministry of Foreign Affairs in September and October 1946 indicate that the employees of the Ministry who were appointed to work as interpreters at the Tokyo Trial (initially, Mori, Jun Tsuchiya, Shimanouchi and Masao Yamanaka) received a monthly salary of JPY1,800 (the equivalent of US$120 at the time), with an additional JPY100 (about seven dollars) per diem. In light of the fact that the Japanese government had established price control regulations with the introduction of the new yen in 1946, and set JPY500 (US$33) a month as the standard cost of living, interpreting at the Tokyo Trial was a relatively well-paying job for Japanese citizens, especially at a time when five million of them were reportedly out of work (see "Shitsugyosha, jissu wa go-hyaku-man ka," *Asahi Shimbun*, January 12, 1946, 3). In fact, the advertisements for interpreters placed in the *Nippon Times* by the occupation forces frequently mention "High Pay."

The Interpreters' Booth

The Tokyo Trial was held in the auditorium of the former Japanese Military Cadet School, in the Tokyo district of Ichigaya, which had been requisitioned by U.S. forces in August 1945. (The auditorium, now called Ichigaya Memorial Hall, is located on the premises of the Japanese Ministry of Defense.) The building, which had once housed the offices of Japanese military leaders, including some of the defendants at the IMTFE, was renovated for the Tribunal by the Japanese government at a cost of nearly JPY100 million (approximately US$6.7 million). According to a report in the *Nippon Times* ("Setting for Coming Big Trials Is Completed," March 23, 1946), as many as 450 Japanese men worked non-stop for three months to complete the project.

Following the design of the courtroom used for the Nuremberg Trial, the Ichigaya courtroom, which was 90 feet by 115 feet, had a raised bench for the eleven justices on the east side, while the accused sat in a box thirty feet away directly facing the bench. Between the accused and the judges' bench on the main floor were the witness box and tables for the prosecutors and the defense counsel. There were other seating areas for the prosecution and defense teams below the stage area and below the defendants' box. The stage area along the south end of the room was used for a motion picture booth and dignitaries were seated just below the booth. Near the auditorium entrance on the north side were seats for journalists: those on the bench side were for the international press and those on the defendants' side were for the Japanese press. More than 250 seats were available in the public gallery on the balcony over the press section. Cinematic lighting was hung from the ceilings for use in the filming of the proceedings.

The *Nippon Times* article cited above includes a photograph of the interpreting equipment (an IBM machine, as discussed below), captioned "a picture of time-saving interpreters' equipment brought here for *possible* use in the trial" (author's emphasis). The wiring seems to have been at least partially available from the beginning of the trial, since (according to *Asahi Shimbun* Hotei-kisha-dan 1948, 57) the Soviet judge and his secretary used headsets to listen to interpretation from English into Russian throughout the proceedings, but to begin with neither the complete headset wiring nor an interpreters' booth had been installed, so during the first month of the trial the interpreters and monitors worked from a table between the witness box and the prosecutors' table on the main floor (as described in "Curtain is Opened on War Crime Trial," *Nippon Times*, May 4, 1946). According to Toshiro Shimanouchi (quoted in Komatsu 2003, 72), the courtroom was noisy and the interpreters had difficulty hearing the proceedings.

Although no official records have been found that clearly describe when the equipment and booths for interpreting became available in the courtroom, some of the documents and photographs indicate that the installation of the equipment took place in phases. Headsets and three-channel buttons seem to have been attached to all the seats in the courtroom during a recess that lasted from May 18 to June 2, 1946. A box-shaped glass cover was also set up on a table at the end of the seating for dignitaries against the stage. An article in another leading Japanese newspaper, the *Yomiuri Shimbun*, reported on the use of the new interpreting system when Chief Prosecutor Joseph Keenan delivered his opening statement on June 4, 1946 ("Nagareru wayaku no chinjutsu," June 5, 1946, 4). A headset was available for every seat in the courtroom, and those present could hear Keenan's statement in English on Channel 1 and the simultaneous delivery of its Japanese translation on Channel 2. The *Nisei* monitors stayed in a "glass box" at the right end of the dignitaries' seating area and took turns reading prepared Japanese translations aloud. Reportedly, there was also a Soviet interpreter ducking her head into a "glass box" at the left end of the seating for dignitaries (*Asahi Shimbun* Hotei-kisha-dan 1948, 57, 291), but it is unknown when this "glass box" for the Russian interpreters was built. An article in the *Nippon Times Magazine* ("Unscrambling Babel," February 27, 1947) refers to it as the "extreme left booth" for "the running translations of the proceedings in Russian" for the Soviet judge.

After the headsets with a channel button and a "glass box" (or two) were put in place, small red lamps were installed during another recess, which lasted from June 5 to June 12 (Fuji 1988, 99–100). They were placed in front of the President of the Tribunal and at the witness box and lectern for the prosecutors and the defense lawyers. A steady light indicated that interpretation was being delivered, while a blinking light indicated a request to the speaker to pause for interpreting.

EXHIBIT 2.1 RYUKICHI TANAKA IN THE WITNESS BOX, JULY 3, 1946, WITH TWO INTERPRETERS (MONITORS) IN A "GLASS BOX" ON THE RIGHT SIDE AT THE BACK

No documents have been located indicating exactly when the full-fledged interpreters' booth (as opposed to a "glass box") was built, but it was probably when the air-conditioning system was also installed during yet another recess, which lasted from July 11 to 14 (Takashi Oka says (2005 interview with the author) that the booth was perhaps built during a recess in June, but a photograph taken on July 5 does not show the booth structure on the stage). Behind the seats for dignitaries, the interpreters' booth was built on the stage, which had been formerly designated for the imperial seat used by Emperor Hirohito when he attended the Cadet School's ceremonial events. According to the official guided tour of the Ichigaya Memorial Hall (as of February 13, 2006), until the end of the war the stairs to the imperial seat had been for the exclusive use of the Emperor, but they were now used by the people who worked in the interpreters' booth and by the judges, who walked behind the booth through the stage to reach the bench during the trial. (Today, the booth and the seats are no longer in the auditorium, but some photographs of the Tokyo Trial are exhibited. Visitors can also walk up and down the stairs to the stage and feel the carved surfaces that were meant to secure the Emperor's steps.)

Exhibit 2.2 The Courtroom

The installation of the interpreters' booth completed the system for delivering interpretation that was used for the rest of the proceedings. According to Takashi Oka (2005 interview with the author), interpreters, monitors and court reporters worked in the booth with no divisions, but the "glass boxes" mentioned above seem to have been used at times. At least one photograph of the proceedings shows the main booth on the stage with a little box-like booth to its left, while the *Nippon Times Magazine* article cited above mentions three "booths" in use during the proceedings in which exhibits were lodged with very few witnesses. All extemporaneous remarks were interpreted in the main booth, prepared translations in Japanese were read simultaneously in the booth on the extreme right, and simultaneous interpretation into Russian was provided from the booth on the extreme left. The default channel arrangement was to use Channel 1 for English and Channel 2 for Japanese, while the third channel was used for Russian interpretation as a stand-alone arrangement for the Soviet judge (Brackman 1987, 213–214; *Asahi Shimbun* Hotei-kisha-dan 1949, 255).This language designation, however, was sometimes adjusted to accommodate a language other than English or Japanese, or certain other types of proceedings, such as when there were no Japanese witnesses or speakers.

Microphones were placed in front of the President of the Tribunal, at the lectern for the prosecutors and the defense counsel, at the witness box and in the interpreters' booth. According to some journalists who observed the proceedings, the microphones were so sensitive that those using headsets could hear interpreters engaging in off-the-record private conversations, turning pages of documents and pouring water into glasses (*Asahi Shimbun* Hotei-kisha-dan 1948, 252; "Nagareru wayaku no chinjutsu," *Yomiuri Shimbun*, June 5, 1946, 4). These oversensitive microphones were sometimes problematic for the interpreters as well. In the article cited above, the *Nippon Times Magazine* reported:

> A cough, a sneeze, the rustling of papers or a whispered conversation caught by the sensitive microphones installed at various places in the courtroom often interfered with reception, and if, as a result, the interpreter is uncertain of what was said, he would have to be covered by his teammate or the monitor. If the latter also are uncertain, then the court reporter on the floor, who usually has better reception, would have to be asked to read back the passage, thus causing a delay.

Despite the availability of the IBM equipment, which was identical to that used at Nuremberg (see Gaiba 1998, 38–40), the predominant mode of interpreting at the Tokyo Trial was consecutive, simply because the Tribunal had come to the conclusion that simultaneous interpretation between English and Japanese was not achievable.

This approach is in contrast to that taken at the first Nuremberg Trial, which is considered a monumental event in the history of simultaneous interpreting. According to Takashi Oka (2005 interview with the author), David Akira Itami, the most competent of the monitors, strongly insisted that simultaneous interpretation between English and Japanese was impossible because of the differences in sentence structures between the two languages. Simultaneous interpreting was used only when the speaker read a document and its translation was available to the interpreter. In effect, this was nothing more than simultaneous reading of a prepared translation, and it was actually delivered by the monitor, not the regular interpreters.

The use of the consecutive mode of interpreting enabled interjections by the monitor who sat next to the interpreters in the booth. As mentioned above, red lamps were used to indicate to the speaker when to start and stop his statement. The transcripts indicate, however, that some speakers were not observant of the lamp signals: they sometimes started speaking before an interpretation was completed or kept talking despite a request to pause (specific examples are given in Chapter 5).

The Interpreters at Work

The Japanese transcripts of the Tokyo Trial show that two to four interpreters were assigned to each morning or afternoon session. According to Takashi Oka (2005 interview with the author), they usually took turns interpreting every thirty minutes, but the soundtrack of the films recorded during the proceedings and the account given by Masakazu Shimada (2000, 22–23) both indicate that they did so in a flexible fashion, under the direction of the monitor, depending on the requirements of a particular procedure and the competence of the assigned interpreters. (Some interpreters interpreted in two directions, Japanese into English and vice versa, others only in one, Japanese into English or vice versa.) The interpreters worked for two days and had the third day off, so each worked for four days every week. The teams were assigned by the chief of the Language Section. According to Shimada (2000, 24), the core members of the team, who worked on a regular basis, were Shimada himself, Oka, Toshiro Shimanouchi and, later, Makoto Taji.

"Unscrambling Babel," the article in the *Nippon Times Magazine* already cited above, presents the work of the interpreters as "mentally exacting, brain-racking, and back-breaking." The interpreters told the reporter that Sir William Webb's statements were the easiest to interpret, since he adhered to his own instruction to the speakers to speak clearly, slowly and in short sentences. In addition to the trouble they had with the French prosecutor Oneto's accent (mentioned above), the interpreters said that they could not understand Ichiro Kiyose, the chief Japanese defense counsel, when he started speaking in English in his opening statement, so he was asked to speak in Japanese and did so from then on. More generally, the interpreters faced problems whenever a speaker used "long-winded sentences when he could not possibly repeat himself," spoke "rapidly, resembling machine-gun fire, or in a diction that clouds the thought" or ignored the flashing red light during a heated discussion. They also had difficulties when lawyers used Latin legal terms or when Japanese speakers cited phrases from the Chinese classics. Finally, they were unsure how to interpret certain ambiguous Japanese phrases, such as "*hai*," which can mean "yes" or "no" depending on the way the question is asked, and how to handle differences in sentence structure between English and Japanese, especially in the position of the verb (which generally comes at the end of a clause in Japanese). Drawing on his interviews with the interpreters, the reporter asserts that the basic requirements for the job are linguistic talent, mental alertness, general knowledge and a good memory, and recommends that the interpreters be briefed by the speakers in advance of any extemporaneous statements. He also refers to the interpreters' view that too much note-taking interfered with their comprehension of what was being said. (All these comments are still relevant today, raising issues that are frequently discussed in professional and training settings.)

One issue that the article does not address concerns the role played in the proceedings by the monitors and the language arbiter. A monitor was usually assigned to each morning or afternoon session, and sat next to the interpreters in the booth. The language arbiter, who sat in the prosecution team's seating area on the main floor throughout the court proceedings, engaged with the court when a dispute or confusion over translation or interpretation arose or when he announced a ruling by the Language Arbitration Board on a disputed translation or interpretation. The following is an example of how the monitors and the language arbiter worked, taken from the transcripts of proceedings on September 11, 1947, during the direct examination of the defendant Sadao Araki, a military and political leader of wartime Japan (IMTFE Transcripts, pp. 28,235–28,236; Kyokuto Kokusai gunjisaiban sokkiroku (Japanese transcripts), 269(3), with author's translation of Araki's remarks):

> McManus [defense counsel]: Then what was it you said that was misinterpreted by the paper, General?
>
> Araki: *Sono jijo o ohanashi sureba, ima no Keizaikai wa kyu ni kite chotto hanashi o shite kure to iu koto de atte, toji tosei-keizai no tame ni geta o hake, hadashi de aruke to iu yo na koto ga atta no de, sayo na koto dewa ju-nen no niju-nen no to choki no koto wa shinbo dekinai .*
> . . .
>
> [The fact is that the Economic Association came to me suddenly and asked me to make a few remarks. At that time, because of the controlled economy, there were calls for people to wear clogs or walk barefoot, and under such circumstances it would be impossible to endure things that would last for a long period, such as ten or twenty years.]

Interpreter: The facts of the situation are as follows: this Political and Economic Research Association came to me suddenly and asked me to make a few remarks. At that time the question of controlled economy was being discussed and it was being advocated that people should go barefoot and wear wooden clogs instead of shoes. In such a state of affairs it would be difficult to conduct a long-range war for ten or twenty years, and it was my opinion that in such a state of affairs a long protracted war, lasting ten or twenty years, Japan could not endure such a protracted war – such an affair. Not war, an affair.

Monitor [David Akira Itami]: Strike out the "war" and just say, with such an idea it would be impossible for Japan to endure an affair which may last ten or twenty years.

President: Who said strike out "war," the witness or the interpreter?

Monitor: The interpreter, sir. That was a correction by the monitor.

President: Did the witness at any time use the word "war?"

Monitor: No, sir.

The following day, the language arbiter, Major Lardner Moore, delivered the corrected version of the interpretation for the record:

If the Tribunal please, I offer the following language corrections: Record page 28,235, line 23, delete from "state" to the end of the paragraph and substitute "case it would be impossible to endure for a long period of ten or twenty years."

Translators and Translation Disputes

The language arbiter was also involved in translation matters. In fact, most of the rulings the arbiter announced concerned errors in the translations of exhibits admitted into the proceedings, rather than errors in interpretation. A brief description of how the translation of documents was handled should provide a fuller picture of how language needs were addressed during the Tokyo Trial.

In accordance with the Tokyo Charter and the Tribunal's rules of procedure, all documents submitted in evidence had to be accompanied by translations into English or Japanese, as the case might be. In addition, any prepared statements addressed to the court, such as the closing arguments and the judgment, had to be translated in advance for the participants as well as for the interpreters and monitors.

A total of about 230 translators, 175 on the prosecution side and 55 on the defense side, worked on an enormous collection of documents, including approximately 30,000 pages of exhibits admitted in evidence. At the conclusion of the trial, the *Nippon Times* (November 14, 1948) reported on the work of the translators for the prosecution and the Tribunal under the headline "200 Language Experts Complete Huge Task":

> The court's nearly 200 language specialists translated 3,195 documents, plus countless other statements, written or spoken in English, Japanese, Chinese, Annamese [that is, Vietnamese], Dutch, French, German, Italian, Malayan, Russian, Spanish, Swedish, Burmese, Marshallese, Mongolian, Solomon Island dialects, and Tho, a language used in northern French Indochina.

Given the sheer volume of the translations and the variety of languages involved, the achievements of these translators should indeed be noted as an outstanding feat in the history of translation.

Securing a sufficient number of translators to work on the exhibits and other types of documents presented a major challenge for all the parties at the Tokyo Trial. *Nisei* linguists were dispatched from SCAP's Translator and Interpreter Service to work as translators for the Tribunal, but the Service's own survey of linguist requirements, dated January 29, 1946, states that "A-rated" translators—those who could "freely and independently translate written Japanese into accurate English and rapidly scan Japanese documents, including those written in styles other than *Kaisho* [block script]"—accounted for only 2.2 percent of the translators employed by the Service at that time. Further, these translators had to work in support of several different activities of the occupation forces besides the IMTFE.

The shortage of translators was especially of concern to the defense counsel. In November 1946, toward the end of the prosecutor's case, the defense attorneys held emergency meetings and requested the Legal Section of SCAP to urgently provide twenty-five translators and five interpreters to help them in preparing their case. The language used in the relevant documents indicates the seriousness and urgency of the problem. For instance, according to a letter from the defense attorneys to a court administrative officer, dated November 25, 1946 (see Smith 1946),

> the defense is confronted with an overwhelming task which
> cannot be discharged without additional personnel . . . it would be
> a tremendous embarrassment to the Supreme Commander, the
> Tribunal and the Defense should the presentation of the case of
> the Defense break down because of inability to process and clear
> those documents without undue delay.

Meirion and Susie Harries (1989, 117) describe how Japanese translators were brought in by Chief Prosecutor Joseph Keenan's team in preparation for the trial:

> Out of a total staff which by January 1946, had swollen to seventy,
> only five could read Japanese, and Keenan had no option but to
> request the Japanese government to supply fifty or so English-
> speaking Japanese nationals—"Hobson's choice," as he put it.
> Eventually some two hundred Japanese nationals were employed
> on the staff of the International Prosecution Section, which may
> have contributed to the constant breaches of security that plagued
> the trial; the British list of proposed defendants, for example, was
> leaked to the press almost as soon as it was notified to Keenan.

The Japanese nationals who worked as translators at the Tokyo Trial were mainly academics and university students, such as those from Tsuda College, a women's university founded by a pioneer female educator, Umeko Tsuda (who had been schooled in the United States). They included Shigeto Tsuru, a Harvard-educated economist who was then working for the Ministry of Foreign Affairs and later became President of Hitotsubashi University; Kazuji Nagasu, a Marxist economist who later became Governor of Kanagawa Prefecture; and Mayumi Moriyama, one of the female student translators, who later became a member of Parliament, Minister of Education and then Minister of Justice.

Yukio Kawamoto was one of the *Nisei* linguists assigned to work as a translator first for the prosecution and later for the defense. When interviewed by the author (in Springfield, Virginia, on March 20, 2005), he talked about how he met his future wife during the trial. When he was working on the translation of the diary of Marquis Koichi Kido, the Emperor's closest adviser, which was to be used as a prosecution exhibit, he found that he could not understand Kido's elegant cursive writing. The Japanese woman who wrote out the diary in standard style for him to translate later married him. Kawamoto's wife and other readers of handwritten Japanese, cursive or otherwise, were known as "examiner–translators," and advertisements in the *Nippon Times* specified that they should be "men or women with thorough knowledge of all types of Japanese writing and good knowledge of English."

The practice of "team translation" is also evident in some accounts of the trial. The translation of Kido's diary had "screener" versions and "exact" versions, suggesting that it was translated in two stages, perhaps by different groups of translators. To take another example, Ichiro Kiyose, one of the defense counsel for Hideki Tojo, translated Tojo's affidavit into English and his U.S. colleague, George Blewett, then edited it (Asahi Shimbun Tokyo saiban kisha-dan 1995, 157). The most systematic team endeavour was the translation of the judgment, which took nearly three months to finish. Nine *Nisei* and twenty-six Japanese translators worked on the 300,000-word document. A professor of international law from the University of Tokyo checked their translation and the head of the Japanese language section of the Ministry of Education edited it for style. These people, together with about thirty stenographers and typists, worked under heavy security in Hattori House, the residence of the President of K. Hattori & Co. (now the Seiko Corporation), and were not allowed to leave the premises for the duration of the project. According to Stephanie Leah Shimada, a granddaughter of the interpreter Masakazu Shimada interviewed by the author (by e-mail and in person in Sunnyvale, California, February 2007), her grandmother and her father visited Shimada once a month while he was working as one of the translators, but saw him only at the gate and were not allowed further on the premises. According to a report in the *Yomiuri Shimbun* ("Tokyo saiban no hanketsu junbi," August 17, 1948), about 120 people, including military policemen, housekeepers and cooks, lived inside Hattori House and were provided with amenities that included a cafeteria, a pharmacy and a library.

EXHIBIT 2.3 TRANSLATORS ARRIVING IN COURT FROM HATTORI HOUSE, AFTER COMPLETING TRANSLATION OF THE JUDGEMENT

There were several hundreds of disputes over the translations that were presented in evidence during the proceedings. According to a document issued by the Language Arbitration Board in May 1948, it handled 433 corrections in response to questions raised by the bench, the prosecution or the defense. For example, on August 28, 1946, one of the defense counsel, Alfred Brooks, pointed out a problem with the English translation of the Japanese term "*nankin-jotai*" (under house arrest) in an exhibit lodged by the prosecution, comprising a telegram concerning how the Japanese Army treated Henry Pu-Yi when he was Emperor of Manchukuo (IMTFE Transcripts, p. 4389):

> Brooks: On the line in here, I think it is one, two, three, four, five, sixth line, on the words "light confinement," there is some question as to the translation from the original telegram, and we would like for the arbiters to check and see if that really means that it was "light confinement" as a prisoner, or if it connotes protective custody. The Japanese characters, as I am told by the Japanese, do not mean that a man is placed as a prisoner status, which "light confinement" might be interpreted by the Court, but it is a different connotation, such as "protective custody," and I think the Court arbiters can check this on the original telegram. That is one thing that is very important on this document especially.

> President: We will ask Major [Lardner] Moore to advise us on the point in due course. Meanwhile, proceed with your further comments.

It seems that Brooks wanted to use language that would imply that Pu-Yi was under the protection of the Japanese Army rather than in confinement. Later in the same session, Brooks took issue with the English translation of the Japanese word "*tsuredasu*" (take away) in another exhibit submitted by the prosecution, concerning the Japanese Army's relocation of Pu-Yi's wife (IMTFE Transcripts, p. 4405):

Brooks: If the Tribunal please, on this exhibit 303, in the fourth line, it reads: "and has attempted to abduct the Empress to Manchuria." The Japanese word used on that line is "*tsuredasu*," t-s-u-r-e-d-a-s-u, and is not the Japanese word "*yukai*," "*yukai*" meaning "to abduct," and "*tsuredasu*" meaning "to take away." I checked that, and I think it is correct. It changes the meaning. I think the context bears out it was not an abduction plan.

President: Like the prior correction, it is not really substantial, but we will have it noted.

It is possible that "take away" and "abduct" would make different impressions on the judges, although Sir William Webb's response suggests that he, at least, saw little difference. Brooks also added follow-up comments on the translation of "*nankin-jotai*" (IMTFE Transcripts, p. 4450):

Brooks: I also checked on Exhibit 297. The word used there—Japanese word there—of the so-called "light confinement" is "*nankin-jotai*," which, as I understand, means "protective custody." It does not mean "as a prisoner"—protecting from someone.

President: Yes.

At the beginning of the morning session the following day, August 29, 1946, the language arbiter, Lardner Moore, announced the ruling of the Language Arbitration Board on the translation of "*nankin-jotai*":

Language Arbiter: If the Tribunal please, I refer to the disputed passage in document 1767-291, exhibit 297. The Japanese term in question, translated literally, would read "condition of light confinement." We recommend that it be rendered "protective restraint" in order to make it harmonize with the context.

President: The correction will be made.

Thus, the defense's suggestion of "protective custody" was rejected and the Tribunal settled on "protective restraint."

This particular correction was announced and recorded relatively quickly once the question had been raised, but in some cases corrections were not announced or reflected in the records in such a timely manner. For example, the correction of the translation of "*tsuredasu*" was not formally recorded until December 26, 1947, one year and four months after the defense had challenged it, and "abduct" was changed to "carry off" (IMTFE Transcripts, p. 36,170).

Such delays, or even omissions, in the making of corrections to translations in the record of the Tribunal caused concerns among some court participants about the lasting impression that incorrect translations might make. For example, in 1977 the Dutch judge B. V. A. Röling, who famously dissented from the final judgment of the Tribunal, commented on a translation error that had troubled him during the proceedings (Röling and Cassese 1993, 53):

> I remember that one document did not fit at all into this development from peace to war. I sent the document to the Translation Office [Language Arbitration Board]. . . . when it came back, it was apparent that previously it had been wrongly translated. The correct translation, made by the official Translation Office, fitted perfectly into its chronological context. So I called upon my colleagues to meet in chambers, and said: I have a problem. We have a document that was wrongly translated. . . . My proposal was to use the correct translation for our judgment. It was refused. We would have had to reopen the session and introduce the correct translation, so they said, because the wrong translation had been used in Court, and that was the evidence that was before the judges. I found that to be utter nonsense, especially as the Japanese had used the Japanese text, the original text, so they had nothing to do with a faulty English translation. I don't know whether the majority opinion made use of the wrong translation, but it would be a silly business to render a judgment on the history of Japan knowing that a wrong translation was used. And it might have had a certain influence on [Baron Koki] Hirota's sentence. . . .

> [First documents] were translated by the prosecution staff. Only if
> a translation was criticized by the defense was it submitted to the
> Translation Office.

The error to which Röling refers is the mistranslation of one of the posts held by the defendant Hirota: "Cabinet Councillor" was mistranslated as "Supreme War Councillor." This error remained uncorrected in the judgment. Incidentally, Hirota was the only civilian among the defendants who were sentenced to death. No historian, however, seems to view this mistranslation as having contributed to Hirota's fate.

The Effects of Interpreting on the Proceedings

The effect of interpreting on the proceedings of the Tribunal has been discussed, though only to a limited extent, by historians and participants, who have generally pointed to three main effects: the relatively extreme length of the trial, which may be attributed to the consecutive mode of interpreting and the frequency of language disputes; the impact of interpreting on the ways in which the lawyers questioned witnesses; and the possible effect of inadequate interpretation on the outcome of the trial.

John Dower (1999, 458) notes that the unavailability of simultaneous interpreting forced the speakers to pause after each sentence until the consecutive interpretation was completed, and refers to comments by a member of the prosecution team (Horowitz 1950, 538) that "the speed of the trial was reduced to one fifth of its normal pace" during the examinations of witnesses. Greg Bradsher (n. d., 180) points to the difficulty of interpretation and translation between English and Japanese, which inevitably meant that a great deal of time had to be spent on resolving language issues.

Robert Barr Smith (1996) argues that the consecutive mode of interpreting and the inadequate language competence of the interpreters "handicapped lawyers for both sides in getting at the truth," because these factors forced counsel to limit their remarks to "short sentences in elementary language." Having to submit documents in advance was also taxing for the lawyers. There were similar problems at Nuremberg: Francesca Gaiba (1998, 101–03) discusses the complaints of lawyers there that they too had to speak slowly for the interpreters and that the spontaneity and momentum of their examinations were lost. The impact of interpreting on lawyers' questioning is often discussed in studies of court interpreting today (see, for example, Berk-Seligson 1990/2002; Hale 2004).

Tatsuoki Shimanouchi (1973, 418–19), who was a member of the defense team, blames the poor performance of the interpreters for Admiral Mitsumasa Yonai's unresponsive testimony on September 22, 1947. He argues that Yonai could not respond properly because he did not understand the Japanese interpretation of the questions. Sir William Webb called Yonai "the most stupid witness I have ever listened to" because of his nonsensical responses (IMTFE Transcripts, p. 28,939). Dower (1999, 467) also refers to the unnatural features of interpreted language, claiming that "the English interpretation tended to be more cryptic than the original statements." Timothy P. Maga (2001, 57) points to the issue of interpreters making a statement more explicit or direct:

> The Japanese language was simply less direct than English. That meant that defendants attempted to "circumvent points," not in an effort to hide guilt, but in the endeavour to answer questions that seemed to them strangely direct. The interpreters themselves would attempt to convey Japanese answers to the Tribunal in the direct manner that the English-speaking lawyers expected. Consequently, the language issue went beyond the bad translation of a word or two.

Noboru Kojima (1971, 50–52) also refers to the Japanese witnesses' avoidance of directness and explicitness in their testimony as being a feature of Japanese language and culture, and argues that this rhetorical style challenged the interpreters, irritated the President of the Tribunal and worked against the Japanese witnesses. Kojima also claims (1971, 257–58) that the *Nisei* monitors' interpretations into Japanese were hard to follow and that their interpolations into English were "too rough," because, in his view, the *Nisei* did not fully understand the nuances of the testimonies by the Japanese witnesses. Kojima believes that the problems with the interpretation disrupted the proceedings, limited the ability of the defendants and their counsel to express themselves and negatively affected the judges' understanding of the testimony. As Dower (1999, 467) states, at the time "no one suggested that translations and interpretations were deliberately skewed or even fundamentally inaccurate," but, according to Kojima (1971, 258), Webb said in an interview after his retirement (as translated by the author from Kojima's Japanese version): "If the Japanese lawyers had been more proficient in English, or the interpreters had been more competent, it might have affected the judgment of the trial."

Nevertheless, no matter how inconsistent the quality of the interpreting might have been at the beginning of the trial, no matter how imperfect the monitors' work might have been and no matter how ineffective the interpreting procedures might have been at the initial stage of the proceedings, a mechanism for correcting errors was in place and operating throughout the trial. The research for this book did not find any incident that would suggest any intentional mistranslation or material error left unchecked during the proceedings. This view is shared by, for example, the former interpreter Takashi Oka (1998, 116). It is therefore very difficult to find any concrete evidence to support Webb's view, as reported by Kojima, on the possible impact of language issues on the outcome of the trial.

CHAPTER 3

PROFILES OF THE LINGUISTS

Given the fact that multiple languages were used by the court participants, the Tokyo Trial could not have been conducted without the work of the interpreters. However, despite the critical role they played in the proceedings, the backgrounds of these linguists, with the exception of David Akira Itami, have remained largely unknown. This chapter focuses on the personal profiles of the main linguists who worked at the Tokyo Trial, in the hope of shedding light on political, social and cultural conditions in Japan and the United States before, during and after the Second World War. (The personal backgrounds of these linguists are also referred to in Chapters 4 and 5.)

The Interpreters

As previously mentioned, only a handful of the twenty-seven interpreters between Japanese and English recorded in the transcripts worked regularly throughout the trial. According to Tomie Watanabe (1998, 10–11), the interpreters who worked most frequently were the following:

Toshiro Henry Shimanouchi	419 sessions
Masakazu Eric Shimada	323 sessions
Takashi Oka	289 sessions
Tomio Mori	216 sessions
Masahito Iwamoto	170 sessions
Makoto Taji	160 sessions
Naoshi George Shimanouchi	61 sessions
Hideo Masutani	69 sessions
Hideki Masaki	55 sessions
Jun Tsuchiya	52 sessions
Masao Yamanaka	42 sessions

More than half of the twenty-seven interpreters were associated with the Japanese Ministry of Foreign Affairs. The rest were Japanese nationals who had grown up in bilingual households and/or with bilingual schooling.

Toshiro Henry Shimanouchi, who interpreted in the greatest number of sessions, was born in Saga, Japan, in 1909 and moved with his family to California in 1912. He grew up in the Japanese communities of San Francisco, Oakland, Livingston, Fresno, and Los Angeles. Until his death in an internment camp, his father was the publisher of the *Nichibei Shimbun*, a Japanese language newspaper, and a well-respected leader in the Japanese American community. After graduating from Occidental College in 1931, Toshiro Shimanouchi could not find work in California because he had not been able to obtain U.S. citizenship, so he moved back to Japan in 1933. After working as a newspaper reporter, he joined the Society for International Cultural Relations, an organization affiliated to the Ministry of Foreign Affairs, as a bilingual staff member. From November 1937 to April 1938, Shimanouchi toured the United States, focusing on the Japanese American community on the west coast, as a lecturer on behalf of the Foreign

Affairs Association of Japan, a semi-official organization with close ties to the Ministry of Foreign Affairs. He undertook this mission in order "to stem the tide of adverse publicity Japan was suffering at the hands of the American press" (Ichioka 2006, 41–42), and defended Japan's activities in Asia. Shimanouchi became an official of the Ministry during the war and in 1951 acted as an interpreter for Prime Minister Shigeru Yoshida at the San Francisco Peace Conference, which negotiated the formal ending of hostilities between Japan and the United States, and the withdrawal of the occupation forces. Shimanouchi had a distinguished career with the Ministry, becoming Consul General in Los Angeles and Ambassador to Norway. After retiring he became a senior adviser to the Japan Federation of Economic Organizations (now the Japan Business Federation). His younger brother, Naoshi George Shimanouchi, also worked for the Ministry of Foreign Affairs, while his son Ken (with whom the author exchanged e-mails about Toshiro in 2007) is currently the Japanese Ambassador to Brazil.

Masakazu Eric Shimada was born in 1912 to a Japanese mother and a German father who was a railway engineer hired by the Japanese government. His father returned to Germany when Shimada was three. He was educated in Japanese schools, but as a child had a lot of exposure to various languages spoken by foreigners in Japan. He studied English writing at a university preparatory school and learned spoken English from a U.S. missionary. While studying in the Faculty of Economics at Keio University in Tokyo, Shimada started working for HAVAS, the French news agency that has since become Agence France Presse (AFP). He also studied French at the Athénée Français in Tokyo and learned to write articles in French through on-the-job training. He was drafted into the Army in 1943, when Japan was already losing ground in the war, but he was placed in the lowest of the three categories of physical fitness for soldiers and never engaged in combat. Instead, he took care of horses in China, procured food and worked as an interpreter for his superiors in Indonesia, after studying the Indonesian language for a few months at a local elementary school. When the war ended, his battalion was in the Talaud Islands of Indonesia, having been deserted by other Japanese troops, and Shimada helped his superior with his English when his battalion was being disarmed and released by Australian troops. Shimada was then separated from the rest of the Japanese soldiers to be treated for a tropical ulcer. Following his recovery, he was hired as a translator on Morotai Island. One of his assignments was as an interpreter at the war crimes trial of ninety-three Japanese personnel on Ambon Island in January 1946. He then landed at Kure in Hiroshima Prefecture with the Australian contingent of the occupation forces, and continued working as a translator and interpreter. After the Tokyo Trial, he received a GARIOA (Government and Relief in Occupied Areas) scholarship to study journalism at Columbia University, where he met Sho Onodera, one of the monitors, who was working in the New York office of a Japanese newspaper at the time. When he returned to Japan, Shimada had a successful career as a journalist with United Press International. He is retired and now lives in Brisbane, Australia, with his daughter Yuri Furuno, who is a translation scholar (and with whom the author exchanged e-mails about her father's career in 2007–08).

Takashi Oka, who was a student at Rikkyo University in Tokyo at the time of the Tokyo Trial, had been born in Tokyo in 1924. His mother, the daughter of a diplomat, had lived in the United States and Canada from the age of twelve to the age of twenty, while his father worked for a U.S. company in Japan. Oka grew up speaking English to his mother and Japanese to his father, and attended a U.S. school in Tokyo from first to fifth grade (ages six to eleven), though he then attended mainstream Japanese high schools. He had to give up on his hopes of going to college in the United States because of the war and instead entered Rikkyo University in 1944. However, he was unable to dedicate much time to his studies because, like other students at that time, he was conscripted to work in a munitions factory and on a farm. He was subsequently enlisted in the Army, but was never sent to the front. After the war, his mother's connection with Haru Matsukata (later the wife of Edwin

Reischauer, a Harvard scholar and U.S. Ambassador to Japan) helped him find work checking Japanese-to-English translations in the Legal Section of SCAP, which was then preparing for the Tokyo Trial. Although he was the youngest interpreter at the trial, he was one of the core interpreters. Afterward, he left Japan to study in the United States and obtained a BA from Principia University and an MA in international and regional studies from Harvard. He was then recruited by the *Christian Science Monitor*, beginning a long and distinguished career as a journalist, not only with the *Monitor* but also with the *New York Times* and *Newsweek*. He retired to live in Washington, DC (where the author interviewed him on December 11, 2005), and had his PhD thesis, "A Political Biography of Ozawa Ichiro: Reformer and Policy Entrepreneur," accepted by the University of Oxford in 2008.

There is not much information available on Tomio Mori. According to documents issued by the Ministry of Foreign Affairs, he was an Embassy Third Secretary when he became one of the three Ministry officials appointed as interpreters in the initial stages of the Tokyo Trial. An article in the *Nippon Times* ("Interpreters Picked For A-Class Trials," April 26, 1946) indicates that his last assignment before the trial had been in Shanghai.

Masahito Iwamoto (see Yamaguchi 1984; Oka 2005 interview with the author; Konosu 2005, 32) was born in Tokyo in 1891 to parents who were both prominent in the Japanese literary world. His mother, Shizuko Wakamatsu, had been educated by a U.S. woman missionary at the Ferris Seminary (now Ferris University in Yokohama), and had become a writer, as well as a translator of English-language works such as Frances Hodgson Burnett's novel *Little Lord Fauntleroy*. His father, Yoshiharu Iwamoto, was a renowned writer and editor who, influenced by New England Protestant ideals, promoted girls' education by heading the Meiji Girls' School and publishing a magazine for women. Iwamoto grew up on the premises of his father's school, which housed foreign teachers as well. After attending Waseda University, he continued his studies at Harvard and met his future wife, Marguerite, who was a Quaker. After returning to Japan and completing compulsory military service, he worked for a British aircraft company, then for the U.S. Navy's office inside the Embassy in Tokyo. After its closure at the outbreak of the Pacific War, he started working for the Domei News Agency, while his wife taught English at Tokyo Woman's Christian University and Tsuda College. According to Takashi Oka (2005 interview with the author), Iwamoto was a traditional man and applied for a post as an interpreter because he wanted to serve the Emperor, who he thought might be called upon to testify at the Tokyo Trial. Iwamoto died in 1975.

Makoto Taji, who became one of the main interpreters for the later stages of the trial, had been raised in a bilingual household with an English mother. According to Oka (2006 email exchange with the author), Taji's English was excellent. After the Tokyo Trial, Taji worked sporadically as an interpreter, and was stationed in the United States in the early 1960s as an interpreter for the Japan Productivity Center. He also worked for a trading company in Kobe. After his retirement he moved to Tokyo to work as a freelance interpreter, but in 1990 he moved again, this time to Thailand, where he died.

Hideki Masaki was an official of the Ministry of Foreign Affairs when he became an interpreter at the Tokyo Trial, having joined the Ministry in 1931, when he was twenty-three years old. His father, Jinzaburo Masaki, a well-known general in the Japanese Army and a member of the "Imperial Way" faction, was arrested after the war as a "Class A" war crimes suspect but was not indicted. Hideki Masaki interpreted for his father during his interrogations, but was not on the team of interpreters when his father testified for the defense at the Tokyo Trial. Hideki Masaki served on and off as an interpreter for Emperor Hirohito between 1959 and 1984, and died in 2001, at the age of ninety-three (see *Togo Senso Jiten*).

Little is known of Masao Yamanaka, apart from the fact that he was Vice Minister of Foreign Affairs—in other words, the highest-ranking permanent official in the organization—at the time of his appointment as an interpreter for the IMTFE.

EXHIBIT 3.1 INTERPRETERS AND MONITORS IN THE BOOTH

The Monitors

The four *Nisei* who served as monitors were David Akira Itami, Sho Onodera, Lanny Miyamoto, and Hidekazu Hayashi (Hayashi worked only sporadically).

Itami, having been the subject of a best-selling novel and a popular television drama series in Japan, has been the most discussed among all the linguists who worked at the Tokyo Trial, and there are a number of books, articles and interviews about him in Japanese (see, for example, Itami 1949/1987; Yamashiro 1984; Kinashi 1985, 2000; Kono 2003; Shimada 2000; Otake 2005). Itami was born in Oakland, California, in 1911, the fourth son of Japanese immigrants. His father had taught English in Japan and had moved to the United States to become a Methodist minister, but he sent all his children to be educated in his hometown of Kajiki, in Kagoshima Prefecture in southwestern Japan. Accordingly, David Akira resided in his aunt's home in Kajiki from the age of three until he was nineteen, becoming an active member of a youth movement known as the Seiunsha, and studying both Japanese martial arts and Chinese classics. Wishing to become a military officer, he applied several times to the Japanese Imperial Army's Preparatory School and to the Naval Academy, but was repeatedly rejected, officially on grounds of ill health, although, according to his friend Kozo Kinashi (2000, 37), Itami speculated that it was really because of his dual citizenship. He failed the entrance examination for the Dai-Shichi Koto Gakko (the Seventh Higher School, now Kagoshima University) and enrolled instead in the Daito Bunka Gakuin (now Daito Bunka University) in Tokyo, an institution that focused on Asian studies and was associated with nationalists and militarists who promoted the ideology of the "Greater East Asia Co-Prosperity Sphere" until the end of the war. However, according to Itami's nephew Makoto Kawakami (interviewed by the author in Ome City, Tokyo, on June 26, 2008), Itami was attracted to Daito because the tuition was free and it offered courses in which he was interested and excelled.

In 1931, after studying Chinese classics, Indian philosophy, and Japanese archery at Daito for three years, Itami abruptly moved back to California, apparently because of his mother's poor health, borrowing the money for the journey from Shigenori Togo, who was also from Kagoshima and was later to be Foreign Minister under Hideki Tojo and one of the defendants at the Tokyo Trial. In the United States, Itami attended a high school and a junior college in Pasadena, studied at Los Angeles City College and worked as a fisherman in Alaska before becoming a reporter on a newspaper aimed at the Japanese American community in California. His father died in 1933 and his mother in 1934, and in 1935 Itami renounced his Japanese citizenship and married a woman who was also *Kibei*.

After the Japanese attack on Pearl Harbor on December 7, 1941, Itami and his family were interned along with nearly 120,000 other Japanese and Japanese American residents on the west coast of the United States. Itami, held at Camp Manzanar, volunteered in June 1942 to teach at the Military Intelligence Service Language School in Minnesota. He later worked in military intelligence in Washington, DC, most notably, deciphering coded conversations, conducted in the dialect of the region where he had grown up, between officials in the Japanese Ministry of Foreign Affairs and diplomats at the Embassy in Berlin. Itami also worked in military intelligence on Iwo Jima. For his intelligence work Itami received the Legion of Merit, the highest medal for non-combatants.

Itami was in Okinawa when the war ended and did not reach Tokyo until November 1945. He joined the Language Section of the Tribunal as a civilian in April 1946 and led the team of monitors throughout the trial. Itami is said to have enjoyed entertaining friends in his home in Washington Heights, a U.S. Army residence in the Tokyo district of Yoyogi, and was also generous with his relatives in Kajiki, sending them money and goods that were scarce at the time. However, when he visited his sick brother in Kajiki in December 1947, some of the locals did not hide their hostility to him as an American. Yet it has also been reported that he was once attacked by Caucasian officers in Washington Heights during a court recess in 1948.

After the Tokyo Trial, Itami stayed on with the U.S. forces as a translator in connection with the Korean War, and also translated Sun Tzu's manual *The Art of War* for General MacArthur. In 1950, however, aged only thirty-nine, he shot himself. His family and friends (see, for example, Kinashi 1985 and Michi Itami quoted in Otake 2005) have since sought to explain his suicide by reference to his experiences as an Asian in the United States and a *Kibei* within the Japanese-American community, as well as the emotional strain he suffered during the trial. Toyoko Yamasaki's novel *Futatsu no Sokoku* (1983; Two Homelands), which is based on Itami's life, was a bestseller in Japan, and a television drama series based on the novel but retitled *Sanga Moyu* (The Mountains and the Rivers Are Burning) was shown on the Japanese public broadcasting station NHK in 1984.

Sho Onodera, who, according to the defense lawyer Tatsuoki Shimanouchi (1973), was a nephew of Admiral Seizo Kobayashi, a governor of Taiwan when it was a Japanese colony, was born in Seattle in 1917 and educated in Japan for seven years before returning to the United States to attend high school. He worked as a sales clerk before being sent to the internment camp at Manzanar, but in June 1942 he left the camp to receive training at the Military Intelligence Service Language School. Given that Onodera was one of Itami's students in the most advanced class there, his Japanese must have been good but probably not at the level of a native speaker in some respects. According to his cousin Yukio Kawamoto (interviewed by the author in Springfield, Virginia, on March 20, 2005), Onodera admired Itami's proficiency in Japanese, especially his mastery of Chinese characters and his deep understanding of Japanese culture. Although Onodera struggled as an interpreter during the Tsuchiya Trial, which took place before the IMTFE began its proceedings (see Chapter 4), his experience as a monitor at the Tokyo Trial seems to have made him sought after as an interpreter for the subsequent trials of "Class B" and "Class C" war crimes suspects in Yokohama. According to Tatsuoki Shimanouchi (1973, 565), the court in Yokohama depended on Onodera so much that it occasionally scheduled its proceedings in accordance with his availability. After these trials, Onodera returned to the United States to attend Oberlin College. He did not obtain a degree there but was hired as a correspondent for a Japanese newspaper and ran its New York office. He also took some acting roles, most notably in the 1974 version of the movie *The Taking of Pelham One Two Three*, until his death in the same year (see IMDb n.d.).

Lanny Miyamoto was born in California in 1921, and had some schooling in Japan, although there is conflicting information on his educational background. The Japanese American Internee Data in the National Archives Database indicates that Miyamoto had five years of schooling between the ages of ten and nineteen and then two years of college in the United States. However, recently declassified information on the U.S. Office of Strategic Services (OSS, the wartime predecessor of the Central Intelligence Agency) indicates that Miyamoto attended Goko College in Japan and then San Jacinto High School in California. Either way, he was a *Kibei* who could speak, read and write Japanese. He worked as a fruit and vegetable packer before being sent to Manzanar and later, in June 1942, being sent to teach Japanese at the University of Michigan. In August 1944, he became a civilian member of the OSS, monitoring and translating radio signals in the Morale Operation Branch in Washington, DC, and then in Calcutta, India. In November 1945 he joined the U.S. Army's bombing survey team. After the Tokyo Trial, he returned to the United States and ran a photography store while teaching judo in the Baltimore area. According to Takashi Oka (2005 interview by the author) and Masakazu Shimada (2000, 24), Miyamoto was the youngest of the monitors and his Japanese seemed rather weak. Oka didn't even know Miyamoto was a *Kibei* until the author pointed that out during his interview in

2005. (It seems that Miyamoto's japanese was so weak that Oka did not even think he had had schooling in Japan.) According to one of his former judo students, Miyamoto died around 2001.

Hidekazu Hayashi was also *Kibei*, although the length of his education in Japan is not known. He graduated from the University of California at Berkeley, eventually landed a job with a major Japanese trading company and worked in New York and Mexico, calling himself "Pancho." During the war, he taught Japanese at the exclusive Japanese language school run by the U.S. Navy at Boulder, Colorado. His name cannot be found in the Internee Data File at the U.S. National Archives but it is included in the Supplementary MIS Register, indicating that he was protected by the Navy from being sent to an internment camp (Slesnick and Slesnick 2006, 93– 94). After working as a monitor at the Tokyo Trial, Hayashi tried to get work as an interpreter for the U.S. State Department but did not succeed in doing so and died shortly afterward.

The Language Arbiters

Two U.S. Army officers served as language arbiters at the Tokyo Trial: Major Lardner Moore until September 1947 and then Captain Edward Kraft.

Moore was born into a U.S. missionary family in Osaka in 1898, and was home-schooled until he went to the United States to study theology at Austin College in Texas. In 1924 he returned to Japan to work as a missionary, but in June 1942, after being briefly interned, he joined the group of foreigners who left Yokohama aboard the *Asama Maru* bound for Lourenzo Marques (now Maputo) in Mozambique. There, in July, they were exchanged with Japanese diplomats and businessmen brought to the African port aboard the *Gripsholm*, a U.S. vessel that then took Moore and others to the United States. En route it stopped in Rio de Janeiro, where Moore's brother, who was already in the U.S. Army, met him and persuaded him to join up too. Lardner then spent the rest of the war in charge of a translation team at a military intelligence centre in Maryland. His service as language arbiter followed but ended when he retired from the Army in September 1947. He then resumed his work as a missionary, eventually becoming President of the Shikoku Christian College in Zentsuji, Kagawa Prefecture, before retiring to Oregon, where he died in 1987.

When Moore's son George, a historian, conducted an interview with his father in 1980, Lardner Moore explained that he was not actively involved in the deliberations of the Language Arbitration Board over disputed translations and interpretations, but his fluency in Japanese did allow him to play an active role during the trial, especially in its early stages. He was essentially a broker between the Tribunal and the linguists (as discussed in Chapter 4), and Sir William Webb seems to have held him in high regard. Moore was also close to Erima Harvey Northcroft, the judge from New Zealand, and some of the other judges, taking them on excursions around Tokyo.

There was one disconcerting incident involving Moore that suggests something of the attitudes to "orientals" that could be held even by Westerners who, like Moore, had spent many years in East Asia. When Henry Pu-Yi was giving evidence, on August 26, 1946, the examining defense counsel asked for a clarification of one of the witness's answers. Moore responded as language arbiter, but the chief prosecutor questioned Moore's ruling by pointing out his unfamiliarity with the Chinese language. Moore then appealed to Sir William Webb (IMTFE Transcripts, p. 4300):

> "Mr. President, since my qualifications have been called in question, I hope the Tribunal will indulge me in saying that I have had thirty years of experience in oriental question and answer; and it is an established fact that an oriental, when pressed, will dodge the issue."

Webb confirmed that Moore did not in fact understand Chinese and then reproved him:

". . . you said a thing which you should not have said. It is quite beyond your province to comment on the nature of evidence given by orientals; and I ask you to withdraw that comment."

Moore apologized to the court but, according to his son (interviewed by the author in Kensington, California in December 2005), he was so upset by the incident that he had to walk around the Imperial Palace (a distance of about three miles) in order to get himself "adjusted" before heading home. In his interview with his son in 1980, he disclosed that the Chinese judge, Mei Ju-ao, wanted to have him removed from the proceedings altogether, but Webb protected him.

After Moore was discharged in September 1947, Captain Edward Kraft assumed the post of language arbiter. Much of Kraft's background remains unknown, but the records of the Military Intelligence Service Language School show that he studied elementary Japanese there for one year, in classes set up for Caucasians who were to assume supervisory positions in the linguist teams, since *Nisei* were not allowed to be commissioned in the U.S. Army at that time. Kraft also took part in the preparatory Japanese language course at the University of Michigan (see Chapter 4), which was also aimed at Caucasians expected to catch up with the *Nisei* they were to supervise.

The Language Section Chiefs

The transcripts of the Tokyo Trial show that there were four active or retired military officers who headed the Language Section at different times. At the time of Hideki Tojo's testimony (discussed in Chapter 5) Marvin Anderson, a retired Marine Staff Sergeant, was chief of the Section. Anderson was born in Little Rock, Arkansas, around 1918. He spent six months in 1942 studying Japanese at the Marines' language school in Samoa and then interrogated Japanese prisoners of war in Guadalcanal, New Caledonia, and Guam until May 1945, when he was assigned to a Japanese language school in

North Carolina. He joined the staff of the Tribunal as a civilian during the second half of the proceedings. After the trial, he married a Japanese woman, and died in Japan in 1954. He is buried in the Foreigners' Cemetery in Yokohama. Having had relatively limited exposure to the Japanese language, Anderson probably did not have a good command of it, and Takashi Oka (2008 email communication with the author), says that he never heard Anderson speak Japanese during the proceedings.

CHAPTER 4

HIERARCHY AND LEARNING PROCESS

Interpreting at the IMTFE presented some remarkable phenomena that have rarely been observed in other interpreting settings. Broadly speaking, there were two major factors that contributed to the uniqueness of the process. The first is that, like the Nuremberg Tribunal, the Tokyo Tribunal was an unprecedented international court where novel language requirements had to be met. The other is the extraordinary circumstance that people who had once worked under the defendants facilitated the proceedings as language mediators. This chapter explores why the three-tier structure for the interpreting system was established, examines the complex and ambivalent standing of the *Nisei* linguists and considers the process of trial and error in the development of the interpreting procedures, focusing on the exchanges between the President of the Tribunal and the personnel of the Language Section during the initial stage of the trial.

The Hierarchical Structure

As has been discussed in the preceding chapters, one of the highly unusual features of the interpreting arrangements at the Tokyo Trial was the presence of three tiers of linguists: a bottom tier of interpreters who were all Japanese nationals, a middle tier of monitors who were all *Nisei*, and a top tier, the Language Arbitration Board, which consisted of one member appointed by the Tribunal to act as language arbiter and one member each appointed by the defense and the prosecution.

The judgment itself provides some explanation as to why this hierarchy was established (see Part A, Section I, "Establishment and Proceedings of the Tribunal," in IMTFE 1948):

> The need to have every word spoken in Court translated from English into Japanese, or vice versa, has at least doubled the length of the proceedings. Translations cannot be made from the one language into the other with the speed and certainty which can be attained in translating one Western speech into another. Literal translation from Japanese into English or the reverse is often impossible. To a large extent nothing but a paraphrase can be achieved, and experts in both languages will often differ as to the correct paraphrase. In the result, the interpreters in Court often had difficulty as to the rendering they should announce, and the Tribunal was compelled to set up a Language Arbitration Board to settle matters of disputed interpretation.

This statement does not, however, explain why the monitors were appointed, or why three different socioethnic groups played three different roles within the interpreting system. In pursuit of an answer, it is necessary to examine the use of interpreters in the two Japanese war crimes trials that took place before the Tokyo Trial.

The first of these was the trial of General Tomoyuki Yamashita, which started in Manila on October 29, 1945, and has since been cited as the origin of the doctrine of "command responsibility" in war crimes cases: Yamashita was charged for not controlling his troops, who disobeyed his order to withdraw and massacred civilians in Manila in February 1945. Yamashita was sentenced to death by hanging on December 7, 1945, and was executed on February 23, 1946. The second of these trials was a U.S. military trial held in Yokohama against Tatsuo Tsuchiya, a former prison guard, from December 18 to December 27, 1945. Tsuchiya was sentenced to life imprisonment for mistreating prisoners of war. In both these trials, interpreters were procured from among U.S. military personnel who were not entirely qualified, and internal correspondence of the U.S. military at the time, as well as a book that one of Yamashita's attorneys published later, indicate that there were serious problems with the interpreting in these proceedings.

For example, on October 27, 1945, it was reported to SCAP in Tokyo (in correspondence now held in the Records of the Allied Operational and Occupation Headquarters, World War II, in Record Group 331 at the U.S. National Archives) that three Caucasian Navy and Marine officers who had been appointed as interpreters for Yamashita's trial had refused to take the interpreters' oath, citing their lack of qualifications in spoken Japanese, and that it might be necessary to "furnish [the] best *Nisei* interpreters available." In response, the Commander in Chief, Army Forces, Pacific, asked on October 28: "Why was competent interpreter personnel not selected in sufficient time to prevent this outrageous failure? . . . You have had 40 A class Linguists to choose from, why were not a sufficient number selected?"

Yamashita had a personal interpreter named Masakatsu Hamamoto, a Harvard-educated civilian who had been attached to the Japanese Army during the war. He was indispensable to the communications that took place outside the courtroom, such as those between Yamashita and his counsel, and in Yamashita's psychiatric evaluations, but he was not permitted to act as an interpreter in court because he himself was also a prisoner of war. Thus, Yamashita's trial was conducted with the help of those *Nisei* linguists who were available and willing to serve. According to A. Frank Reel (1971, 145–46), who was one of Yamashita's defense attorneys,

> the official court interpreters were divided into two groups—American *Nisei* soldiers, whose Japanese was fairly good when restricted to elementary or "kindergarten" expressions, but whose English left much to be desired, causing them frequently to take liberties in altering counsel's questions to fit their knowledge of the languages, and a number of American naval and marine officers, whose English was excellent, but whose Japanese was spotty and required constant use of translation dictionaries.

This account is confirmed by Sueo Ito, one of the seven *Nisei* interpreters who worked at Yamashita's trial (and whom the author interviewed by telephone on January 14, 2006). Ito, a Hawaiian *Nisei*, recalls that he had studied only military Japanese and never learned standard Japanese during his nine-month training at the Military Intelligence Service Language School. He admits that he had difficulty interpreting legal terms and had to consult dictionaries all the time.

To address these problems, Hamamoto was permitted to sit beside Yamashita during the trial and conduct "whisper interpreting" from English into Japanese. Reel (1971, 145–46) comments that "this was a *tour de force* of stupendous proportions that had the effect of shortening the proceedings by many weeks, for, without Hamamoto, the court interpreters would have had to translate the entire trial for the accused." However, Hamamoto was not allowed to interpret Yamashita's testimony into English for the court, so Yamashita requested Ted Yajima, the best *Nisei* interpreter at the trial, to interpret his testimony. Concerned about

Yajima's competence nonetheless, Yamashita said to him before he took the witness stand: "Yamashita wants no mistakes. On long sentences I will repeat them twice. Listen carefully—with the brain as well as with the ear" (Reel 1971, 146). In addition, discussions over disputed translations took up much of the time of the court. There was even an incident in which newspaper reporters who had pointed out interpreting errors were called to testify in court and elaborate on their opinions (Reel 1971, 45–49).

Exhibit 4.1 Hamamoto (middle) interpreting for Yamashita (right) during his trial in Manila

Tsuchiya's trial in Yokohama was also disrupted by interpreting problems. According to Timothy P. Maga (2001, 15–16), the defense attorney complained about the inaccuracy of the official interpreters' work, and some of the mistakes made caused laughter and disturbance in the courtroom, such as Tsuchiya's nickname, "Little Glass Eye," being rendered as "Big Glass Eye" or "Big Glass Tooth"; "a stick" and "a club" both being used for the same Japanese word; and confusion stemming from the fact that Japanese nouns generally show no distinction between singular and plural, as when it became unclear whether one soldier or several soldiers beat up prisoners. The chief interpreter was Sho Onodera, a *Nisei* linguist who became one of the monitors at the Tokyo Trial. He later "admitted that his task was a difficult one, for much of the 'pedestrian Japanese and English' used at the trial was 'virtually impossible' to translate directly" (Maga 2001, 15).

While the trials in Manila and Yokohama were experiencing these problems, the International Prosecution Section was being established and the Tokyo Charter was being prepared. Documents that explicitly link the interpreting problems in Manila and Yokohama to the Tribunal's decision to open up its recruitment of interpreters to Japanese nationals have not been located, but internal military correspondence (now held in the Records of the Allied Operational and Occupation Headquarters) clearly suggests that the Legal Section of SCAP was aware of the problems. The IMTFE could not be seen to have the same problems, given that it was an international forum and not a U.S. military court and that it was to attract close attention from all over the world.

As has been previously discussed, many of the interpreters at the Tokyo Trial were employed by the Ministry of Foreign Affairs, one was the son of a "Class A" war crimes suspect, two were former soldiers, and at least one (Iwamoto) was concerned about the preservation of the Japanese imperial house. In effect, they were interpreting in proceedings in which their former superiors' lives were at stake. Accordingly, it is conceivable that the Tribunal decided to appoint monitors and arbiters because it was concerned about its interpreters' capacity to act impartially and was loath to appear dependent on citizens of a defeated nation. Documents explicitly stating such concerns have not been found, but two former interpreters, Masakazu Shimada (2000) and Takashi Oka (in interviews with this author), both support this inference. According to Shimada (2000, 20–21), the Language Section selected four *Nisei* to supervise the Japanese interpreters because the chief of the

Section did not himself understand Japanese. In addition, the fact that all the prepared translations, such as the opening and closing arguments, and the judgment, were rendered by the *Nisei* monitors rather than the Japanese interpreters indicates the Tribunal's preference for using non-Japanese whenever it could. As Shimada comments (2000, 34)(the author's translation):

> It was a given from the beginning, and it was expected. Whether it is the judgment or something else, it's the Americans who should be interpreting. Everything! But because they were not competent, Japanese were hired. . . . There were no such [capable American] people. Something formal, like the arraignment—things that were presented at the beginning and the end of the trial—were prepared in writing beforehand. They were translated, Japanese lawyers checked them, and Americans read [them aloud]. So, we never said anything like "Tojo, death by hanging!"

As cited in the judgment, the Language Arbitration Board was established as a "referee" to settle disputes over translations and interpretations. When a translation or interpretation was challenged by the defense or the prosecution, the President of the Tribunal referred the matter to the language arbiter. After deliberation among the board members, outside the courtroom, the language arbiter announced the ruling in the next court session. According to George Moore's interview with his father Lardner Moore (in 1980), the first of the two language arbiters, a naturalized Japanese American lawyer represented the prosecution, and a Japanese citizen who had been the editor of an English-language magazine represented the defense. Moore let these two members of the board discuss and agree on the rulings, and merely reported their decisions to the court. Lardner Moore recalled that his successor, Captain Edward Kraft, was more involved in the board's deliberations and "had his own ideas about what's to be done," even though he had a lower level of competence in the Japanese language. (Kraft's activities during the testimony of Hideki Tojo are examined in Chapter 5.) The Language Arbitration Board probably served to minimize the time spent discussing interpreting and translation disputes in court, and it is also likely that the language arbiter kept an eye on the monitors, all of whom, being *Kibei*, suffered even greater prejudice than other Japanese Americans (see, for example, Kono 2003; Ichioka 2006).

Tomie Watanabe (2000) presents the view that the monitors were appointed primarily to ensure the accuracy of interpretation and that the monitors and the interpreters worked as a team. Masakazu Shimada (2000, 23) mentions that the monitors helped the interpreters by taking notes of numbers and so on. However, the transcripts and the soundtrack of the films made at the Tribunal indicate that there were a number of erroneous "corrections" and arguably unnecessary rephrasings by the monitors. Shimada (2000, 23) also claims that "it was only Mr. Itami [we] depended on. Other monitors may have helped us with dates and such, but they were not capable of correcting errors in interpretation into English, or omissions (the author's translation)." Takashi Oka (2005 interview by the author) was also sceptical of Lanny Miyamoto's competence in Japanese and in fact never realized that Miyamoto was *Kibei*. Asked if he believed that the monitors were needed in order to achieve a higher level of accuracy, Oka (2006 email correspondence with the author) answered (the author's translation):

> Whether or not the monitoring was needed has nothing to do with interpreting. It was a political matter. In a nutshell, [the Tribunal] didn't fully trust the Japanese interpreters, and that's why the monitors and the Language Board were established.

The Complex Standing of the *Nisei* Linguists

Most of the U.S. linguists who worked as monitors and language arbiters for the Tribunal, and as translators and interpreters for the prosecution and the defense, had studied at the Japanese language schools operated by the Army and the Navy during the war. An examination of the historical backgrounds of these language schools should shed some light on the development of U.S. language policy in the context of national security.

Even before the Japanese attack on Pearl Harbor, a division of the U.S. Army on the west coast had started training military intelligence personnel in the Japanese language in preparation for an anticipated war. This classified school was opened in the Presidio of San Francisco on November 1, 1941, with four Japanese American teachers and sixty students, fifty-eight of them *Nisei* and two of them Caucasian. After six months of intensive training, most of the forty-five graduates were sent to various theatres of war to work in intelligence, while some of them stayed on as instructors.

Soon after the attack on Pearl Harbor, all Japanese Americans were reclassified as "4-F," that is, physically, mentally or morally unfit for military service, and later as "4-C" Enemy Aliens, not acceptable for military service because of nationality or ancestry. Almost all the 5,000 *Nisei* in the military were discharged or forced to engage in menial labour, and in February 1942 President Roosevelt signed Executive Order 9066, which resulted in the forced relocation of nearly 120,000 Japanese and Japanese Americans on the west coast to internment camps. By that time, however, the valuable contributions made by the first graduates from the school had been reported back from the front and the Army was becoming acutely aware of the need for more *Nisei* linguists for military intelligence. The school was reorganized under the direct supervision of the War Department and reopened in Minnesota on June 1, 1942, as the Military Intelligence Service Language school. The government then started recruiting several hundred *Nisei* directly from the internment camps to be trained at the School, while continuing to detain their families and friends as enemy aliens. More than 6,000 *Nisei* received six months of rigorous language training and were sent mainly to the Pacific to serve as interrogators, translators, interpreters, codebreakers and "cave flushers" (talking Japanese civilians and soldiers out of their hiding places in caves on Okinawa and other islands). Some of them were seconded to the Navy, as it did not accept *Nisei* enlistments and its Japanese schools (discussed below) had not produced many competent linguists. *Nisei* linguists were also indispensable during the occupation of Japan, which is why enrolment at the Military Intelligence Service Language School actually peaked after the war. The focus of instruction was shifted from military to civilian language and Japanese culture, and more than 5,000 *Nisei* linguists were sent to work in occupied Japan, in intelligence, disarmament, education and finance. Some of them participated in the U.S. contributions to the drafting of the new Japanese Constitution and the formation of the National Police Reserve, which later became the Japanese Self-Defense Forces.

The U.S. Navy took a different approach, recruiting only Caucasians for its Japanese language schools at the University of California at Berkeley and at Harvard, from October 1941, and then at the University of Colorado at Boulder after the forced relocation of Japanese and Japanese Americans, including the schools' instructors, from the west coast. A branch school was established in Stillwater, Oklahoma, in July 1945. One group of students was made up of those who had been born and raised in Japan or China as members of missionary or business families, and the other was made up of those who were "language-oriented *Phi Beta Kappa* college graduates who might be able to learn Japanese quickly" (Slesnick and Slesnick 2006, 2). After one year of intensive training, graduates were commissioned, apparently regardless of their Japanese proficiency (see, for example, Keene 2008), and started working in interrogation, code-breaking, translation, interpreting and other language-related capacities. Later, a number of these "Boulder boys" had careers as Japan specialists in academia, the U.S. Foreign Service, the intelligence community, and the business world (Slesnick and Slesnick 2006, 307–35), most notably two of the "Godfathers of Japanese Studies," the late Edwin Seidensticker, who translated *The Tale of Genji* and works by the Nobel laureate Yasunari Kawabata into English, and Donald Keene, Professor Emeritus of Japanese Literature at Columbia University.

All four of the *Nisei* who worked as monitors during the Tokyo Trial had lived in the United States between the two world wars, a very difficult period for Japanese Americans, especially after the Immigration Act of 1924, which banned further immigration from Japan and made it much more difficult for those who had already immigrated to obtain U.S. citizenship and employment. For many of them, the only jobs available were as "houseboys, gardeners, and fruit and vegetable salesmen" (Michi Itami, quoted in Otake 2005), and even those who had received higher education tended to be restricted to working within their own communities. The monitors were *Kibei*, who as a subgroup of *Nisei* had generally faced even harsher treatment because of their prior experience and education in Japan, which put them "out of step with their *Nisei* peers" (Niiya 2001, 243) and exposed them to prejudice within the Japanese American community itself (see, for example, Niiya 2001; Kono 2003; Otake 2005). However, the problem for the U.S. military, seeking reliable interpreters amid a general atmosphere of extreme hostility to Japanese Americans after the attack on Pearl Harbor, was that

> the vast majority of *Nisei* were too thoroughly Americanized. Of the first 3,700 men interviewed [by the military], only 3 percent proved to speak Japanese fluently. The next 4 percent could be considered fairly proficient in the language. Another 3 percent knew just enough so that they could be thrown into intensive training; only one *Nisei* in ten understood a useful amount of his ancestral tongue. And even the best of them had to be taught military vocabulary and usage. Almost invariably the best qualified were *Kibei*, thanks to their education in Japan. Ironically, they as a group had been the first to be condemned as potentially the most likely to be disloyal. (Hosokawa 1969/2002, 37)

Thousands of *Nisei*, including several hundred from internment camps, volunteered to go to the Military Intelligence Service Language School to teach or train for military intelligence, largely in order to prove their loyalty to the United States. For some

Nisei, it was the only way to escape the dreadful life of the camps (McNaughton 2006, 106), and they took it despite the continuing effects of prejudice within the Army and the Navy (as discussed above). James McNaughton (2006, 130) describes the *Nisei* view of their situation as follows:

> This discrimination rankled the *Nisei*. From their point of view, the War Department did not trust them enough to grant them commissions as second lieutenants. It was especially grating for the college *Nisei*, who felt they met all the qualification for commissioning but one—race.

In fact, the *Nisei* linguists were kept out of most signals intelligence work because of security considerations (McNaughton 2006, 214–19), and Caucasian leaders of language teams "were secretly instructed to keep an eye on their *Nisei* enlisted men while overseas, to make sure they were translating and interpreting accurately, and not providing misleading or false information" (McNaughton 2006, 115; see also the videos oin the website of Military Intelligence Service Resource Center). A document, dated August 24, 1944, in the OSS files on the monitor Lanny Miyamoto also reveals the security concerns that the U.S. government had in connection with using *Nisei* linguists:

> Subject would ordinarily be Security Disapproved, and the possible dangers attendant on his employment are fully known to this office as well as to the branch heads. However, because of the dearth of educated Japanese having the required qualifications, and after satisfactorily investigating the physical security that will surround his work in a highly supervised Japanese group, limited security is recommended on the following terms:

> 1. Subject will only be used in the following activities: Translating or radio monitoring; advising on various phases of Japanese life, customs, policies, politics, etc.; writing and editing Japanese propaganda in suitable manner, or broadcasting such material.

All such activities are to be under the strictest supervision, and all material written, recorded or broadcast by any such employee is to be carefully censored before being disseminated.

2. All work, in the U.S. and in the field, will be done in properly secured areas designated for Japanese personnel and approved for that purpose by the Security Officer in charge, and under supervision.

3. Subject shall not have access to any classified material except as it may be necessary in order for him to properly perform the particular work assigned to him.

4. Subject shall not be given knowledge or information of any overall plans, or of how the material prepared is to be used, except where such knowledge is necessary to affect [sic] the desired result.

This document, which was declassified in August 2008, clearly indicates that the U.S. government recognized its dependence on the language and cultural skills of the *Nisei* linguists but sought to determine the scope of their involvement and to monitor their activities as strictly as possible.

Despite their adversities and the suspicion of disloyalty, *Nisei* served extremely well in military intelligence and earned recognition for their valuable contributions. An article in the *Nippon Times* (November 22, 1945) reported, under the headline "*Nisei* Played Vital Role as Eyes, Ears of U.S. Army," that

the successful training of the *Nisei* had upset the boast of Japanese leaders that the Japanese writing of "*gyosho*" [semi-cursive style] and "*sosho*" [cursive style], as well as the difficulties of the language itself, would completely secure Japanese military documents against deciphering.

Another article in the same newspaper ("Loyalty of *Nisei*, Who Played A Vital Role In Pacific War, Hailed by Their Commander," May 11, 1946) quoted Lieutenant Colonel John E. Anderton, who, when receiving the Legion of Merit for his service in directing Japanese linguists, praised the 800 *Nisei* who had worked under him:

> We didn't have a single instance of disloyalty among the 800 Japanese American boys under my command during three years of fighting against the homeland of their ancestors.... This is remarkable when it is recalled that approximately 94 percent of all intelligence in the Pacific went through the hands of these *Nisei*. They also get another record [that] I believe is unequalled. During the two and a half years the 800 *Nisei* were stationed in Brisbane, there was not a single court martial among them, not a single case of being absent without leave, not a single case of drunkenness nor a single case of venereal disease.

Colonel Sidney F. Mashibir, who had been commander of the U.S. Army's Translator and Interpreter Service in the Pacific, wrote in similar terms in his autobiography (as quoted in Hosokawa 1969/2002, 399):

> Had it not been for the loyalty, fidelity, patriotism, and ability of these American *Nisei*, that part of the war in the Pacific which was dependent upon intelligence gleaned from captured documents and prisoners of war would have been a far more hazardous, long-drawn-out affair. The United States of America owes a debt to these men and to their families, which it can never fully repay.

Along with General MacArthur's statement that "never in military history did an army know so much about the enemy prior to actual engagement" (cited in Niiya 2001), the following remark made by General Charles Willoughby, MacArthur's intelligence chief, is often quoted (for example, in Bradsher 2006, 161):

> The *Nisei* saved one million American lives and shortened the war by two years.... they collected information on the battlefield, they shared death in battle.... in all they handled between two and three million Japanese documents. The information received through their special skills proved invaluable to our battle forces.

A number of testimonials by the *Nisei* linguists themselves discuss both their pride in having proved their loyalty to the United States and their sense of humiliation, resentment and ambivalence about having been sent to internment camps by the same government that later used them in the war against the country of their parents (see, for example, videos available at Densho Digital Archive and Military Intelligence Service Center). Yukio Kawamoto, who worked as a translator at the Tokyo Trial, told the author (in an interview in Springfield, Virginia, on March 20, 2005) of the resentment he felt when he was sent to the Pacific from the Military Intelligence Service Language School while his parents were still being detained:

> I was mad at the government at that time. They treated us so terribly.... My parents were in Utah, in the middle of nowhere, for a whole three and a half years. My I.D. card, what they called a dog tag, the home address was 57A, Topaz, Utah.

James McNaughton (1994) provides the following insight into how these *Nisei* linguists may have viewed their opponents, the Japanese:

> Whether translating captured diaries or radio messages, or interrogating prisoners of war, they had to confront issues of identity and heritage in ways that most other American soldiers could not even imagine. Although, for most of them, learning the Japanese language was a major challenge, involving six months of hard work, the knowledge and appreciation of Japanese culture and society [that] they had absorbed from their parents and upbringing gave them a unique perspective on the enemy they faced. They had a capacity, all too rare at that time, for seeing their opponents as human beings, rather than animals.

Some of the linguists even had brothers and other relatives serving in the Japanese Army, and there are stories of *Nisei* running into relatives on the battlefield, or themselves being mistaken for Japanese soldiers. Some of them also worked for the investigation teams surveying the damage caused by the atomic bombs in

Hiroshima and Nagasaki. Hiroshima was the Japanese prefecture that had produced the most emigrants to the United States, and many of the *Nisei* were distressed by the dropping of the atomic bomb. One *Kibei* linguist found out that his brother was a victim of the bombing when he served in occupied Japan (NHK 2006). Some *Nisei* linguists may have felt guilty about working to defeat the country of their parents (Inouye, quoted in Bigham 2003, 25), and while they were concerned about their families and friends in the internment camps, they were also concerned that their relatives in Japan might be persecuted because of their connections, and had their own fears of being tortured as traitors if they were caught by the Japanese (NHK 2006).

It was, then, in difficult and complex circumstances that David Akira Itami, Sho Onodera, Lanny Miyamoto, and Hidekazu Hayashi arrived in occupied Japan and started working as monitors at the Tokyo Trial. All four of them had experienced the Emperor-centred nationalist education system of pre-war Japan, the forcible relocation to an internment camp (excluding Hayashi), and activities in military intelligence on behalf of a government that still officially regarded them as enemy aliens.

Trial and Error in Establishing Interpreting Procedures

As has been described in Chapter 2, the interpreters at the Tokyo Trial were bilingual Japanese who were called upon to interpret without any prior training. The judges and counsel were equally inexperienced in the use of interpreting in court, and the Tribunal, encountering a number of problems in the course of the proceedings, established its interpreting procedures through a process of trial and error. Since the consecutive mode of interpreting was used, it was possible for participants to stop the proceedings and discuss the issues raised, and the transcripts contain a large number of discussions of interpreting procedures, especially during the first year of the trial. This section examines some examples of these discussions.

On May 3, 1946, the day the proceedings began, one of the Japanese counsel made an extemporaneous remark that the interpreter on duty found difficult to interpret. Ensign David Hornstein, the chief of the Language Section, informed Sir William Webb, the President of the Tribunal, that the interpreter "cannot interpret counsel's speech unless he pauses when directed" (IMTFE Transcripts, p. 48), but Webb did not address the matter.

On May 6, Hornstein joined Major Lardner Moore, the language arbiter, in trying to impress upon Webb the Language Section's request that speakers wait until the interpretation was completed, as the interpreters were not being given enough time to interpret and some remarks were not being interpreted (IMTFE Transcripts, pp. 109–10)

> Language Arbiter: Mr. President, there has been a formal request, sir, from the Language Section Chief that we take a few moments for translation. We have had four remarks, none of which have been put into Japanese for the benefit of the defendants.
>
> The President: Well, I do not see why you should not put into Japanese, for the defendants, a summary of those remarks. If we are going to wait until every word we say is interpreted, this trial will go on for years. There will be a lot of argument. Has every counsel and every Member of the Court to stop at the end of every sentence in the course of a debate while the translation proceeds?
>
> Language Section Chief: Mr. President, if I may, I quote Section III, Article 9, Paragraph b of the·[Tokyo] Charter:
>
>> Language. The trial and related proceedings shall be conducted in English and in the language of the accused—
>
> The President: That does not prevent a summary.

Language Section Chief: That shall be our practice in the future, sir.

The President: Unless the counsel for the defense object, I suggest that that which we have been discussing be summarized. That will be sufficient.

In the end, the matter was settled by the intervention of defense counsel and of Chief Prosecutor Joseph Keenan (IMTFE Transcripts, pp. 110–11):

Major Warren [defense counsel]: If the Court please, we know that at a later time better facilities will be provided where there will be a simultaneous interpretation, but, in order that the record be kept straight—we know [that] some of these accused do not understand English—we feel [that], if you will bear with us in this proceeding, when we again convene the mechanical facilities will be sufficient, and this will be overcome.

Keenan: The prosecution joins in that request and feels that, since, during all this time, there have been translations currently given, there will occur but little delay in having these translations completed at the end of this proceeding; and we agree that, when the formal taking of testimony begins, we will have facilities that will permit quicker current translations.

Webb then had the court reporters identify what parts of the statements had not yet been interpreted into Japanese.

On May 14, the interpreters were struggling because the speaker, Major Blakeney, a defense counsel, was reading a prepared statement and neither the full text of the statement nor its Japanese translation was available to them. The transcripts suggest that many parts of the statement were not interpreted at all. Blakeney was pausing for the interpreters, but Webb suggested that he complete his statement without pauses. In response to Hornstein's remark that the interpreters did not have access to Blakeney's text, or to a translation of it, Webb said, "Well, this interpreter has no difficulty in reading passage for passage. I do not see why he cannot string them all together" (IMTFE Transcripts, p. 204). Blakeney continued, but the interpreter's incomplete and inaccurate renderings of his statement caused disruption. Moore interjected with an explanation of "the inherent difficulties in the Japanese language, which speaks in an opposite way from the English," but Webb ignored his explanation and said, "Well, I cannot understand yet why he can interpret paragraph for paragraph . . . and yet not be able to string those paragraphs together" (IMTFE Transcripts, p. 216). Moore then suggested that the interpreters be provided beforehand with translations of prepared statements, and Hornstein conveyed a request from the defense team for "a complete and accurate translation verbatim," rather than a summary. The discussion continued as follows (IMTFE Transcripts, pp. 217–20, 247–48, and 279–80):

The President: What is to prevent that interpreter from reading as he read before?

Language Section Chief: What he read before, sir, was a summarization of ideas. It contained a certain amount of inaccuracies. We had intended to proceed with that course. Japanese counsel, as I said, has requested a complete and accurate and verbatim translation of Major Blakeney's remarks.

The President: He has been translating some passages, some large and some small. Now he is faced with a translation of a very large passage, put it that way. It covers every page, but he should be able to do it.

Language Section Chief: He can, sir, in a summarization way. But he cannot do it verbatim.

The President: We may be able to meet the wishes of the defense later.

... The President: This translation, of course, is not required to be sure there will be no miscarriage of justice likely. The whole purpose of this translation into Japanese language is to carry out the Charter, which, I think, is public information. The defendants concerned cannot be smarting under any injustice in the circumstances. Their own counsel made the speech. I think, under the circumstances, we should be satisfied if later on the full address delivered by Major Blakeney is given to the defense, and that we should now proceed to hear the reply to the motion ...

... Mr. Kiyose (Japanese defense counsel): The ruling made by the Honorable Judge is highly satisfactory, but, good or bad, unless the proceedings are understood by both the defendants and their Japanese counsel, this cannot be considered a fair trial.

The President: The necessary translations will be provided at the earliest possible moment. I can do no more than direct that. Now, that closes the matter.

On May 15, however, in response to persistent requests from defense counsel, Webb finally acceded to sentence-by-sentence interpreting (IMTFE Transcripts, pp. 305–06):

Captain Coleman [defense counsel]: The Japanese defense counsel asked me to present to the Tribunal their request that the proceedings be conducted in the manner employed the day before yesterday, at which time the translation of remarks was given in Japanese, to be heard by both the defendants and their Japanese counsel. ... Now the Japanese counsel are not in a position to make proper objections at the necessary times or otherwise function as counsel at this trial. This change is considered essential to the conduct of a fair trial. ...

The President: ... Of course, we shall revert to the procedure of the day before yesterday as soon as that is possible. But we also

accede to the request of Captain Coleman, who, we understand,
now represents all accused, to have the short sentences translated
sentence by sentence.

On July 23, the use of relay interpreting involving a third language
became an issue when the first Chinese-speaking witness testified
(discussed in Chapter 2). In response to the Japanese lead counsel's
complaints about incomplete interpretation due to the complexity
of relay interpreting with Chinese, Webb said (IMTFE Transcripts,
pp. 2405–2406):

> Well, as I explained before, all this interpretation of every word
> is not required in the interests of justice. It is required in the
> interests of propaganda. That is the whole point. This elaborate
> system of interpreting every word does not obtain in any national
> court. We try murderers there. We try men who cannot speak
> the English language, but we do not have all of this interpreting. I
> would like the Japanese to understand that. The Charter really is
> mostly concerned with the Japanese people understanding what is
> happening in this Court. It is not required in the interests of justice.

There is no record in the transcripts of any formal objection to
this statement, but it appears that further discussion took place
outside the courtroom, for on July 25 Webb told the court (IMTFE
Transcripts, p. 2478):

> The Chief Referee of the Language Section [Lardner Moore] saw
> me today and complains that, on account of the unnecessary length
> of some of the questions, it is most difficult for the interpreters to
> perform their duties. Some of the passages from the Lytton Report,
> if not the whole report, have already been translated into Japanese
> and, if the translation were made available to the interpreters, their
> duties would not be so difficult. The interpreters are also having
> difficulty with questions which are [in] negative form, although
> they could be in affirmative form. I again urge counsel to make

their questions short and clear, and to give due notice of any passage from a report or other document which they desire to be read to a witness.

On August 19, when Chief Prosecutor Keenan, prompted by a bilingual colleague, pointed out an interpreting error, Webb asked for clarification from the interpreter. Observing the interpreter being pressed, Moore said, "I beg the indulgence of the Tribunal, sir, to respectfully state that any question of the translation in open court simply puts an added burden on the translators and is irritating to them," and offered his own explanation of the error (IMTFE Transcripts, p. 3981). This incident indicates Moore's appreciation of the difficult task of interpreting and his effort to protect the interpreters.

On October 11, based on a discussion he had had with Moore the day before, Webb stressed to the court the following three points: "We should all speak into the microphone, speak slowly, and speak in short sentences if possible" (IMTFE Transcripts, p. 8776). Later, in response to a prosecutor's complaint about being stopped by the interpreter, Webb said, "Our very efficient translators are always doing their best. . . . They have a most difficult task and they are doing it admirably. That is the opinion of the Tribunal" (IMTFE Transcripts, p. 9178). Five months after the beginning of the trial, Webb had become more appreciative of how interpreting works and how difficult it can be, presumably as a direct result of the persistent requests and patient explanations from the Language Section, in particular from Lardner Moore.

Almost a year after the Tribunal convened, Webb stopped showing any sign of unfamiliarity with interpreting or of impatience with the interpreters. On April 29, 1947, for example, he requested that "all documents, including running commentaries of counsel, be presented to the Language Division forty-eight hours in advance in order to insure [sic] simultaneous interpretation, and that the Language Division be notified in advance of any deviations from the planned order of presentation" (IMTFE Transcripts, p. 21,281).

Considerable efforts seem to have been made to respond to these requests. A memorandum to Webb from Colonel Vern Walridge, the General Secretary of the Tribunal, dated May 8, 1947 (and now in the Records of the Allied Operational and Occupation Headquarters, World War II, Records Group 331 in the U.S. National Archives), indicates that Webb was immediately notified of any violation of these procedures (see Walbridge 1947):

1. The Language Division, International Military Tribunal for the Far East, reports that Mr. [William] Logan of the Defense Section failed on the morning of 8 May 47, to inform the Language Division of a change in the planned order of presentation of evidence. The Division was not notified that the witnesses Shoichi Amano and Sadao Ushijima were to be called, and they were not supplied affidavits of the said witnesses.

2. This is in violation of the order as stated by the President of the International Military Tribunal on Friday, May 2, 1947, Page 21,281 of the Record.

Webb replied (in a note also kept in Records Group 331): "As soon as any violation of the Tribunal's order takes place, the officer concerned should report to the President, even if he is then presiding in Court." This indicates that Webb was now eager to address the interpreters' needs and to enforce compliance with the established procedures.

As has been illustrated, there was a great deal of trial and error in the establishment of the interpreting procedures during the initial stages of the Tokyo Trial. In particular, Moore and Hornstein, on behalf of the interpreters, communicated to the court the challenges the interpreters faced and their requests for better procedures, and defense counsel also complained. The procedures eventually settled on included requirements that speakers break their remarks into short segments, that interpreters provide full interpretation, not summaries, and that translations of prepared statements be provided to the interpreters beforehand. Thus, both the interpreters and the users of their services had to come to terms with each other's expectations, requirements, challenges and constraints. It was a learning process for all those facing the unprecedented language issues at the Tokyo Trial.

EXHIBIT 4.2 SIR WILLIAM WEBB IN THE MIDDLE ON THE BENCH

CHAPTER 5

TOJO'S TESTIMONY

This chapter describes and analyzes the behaviour of the interpreters, monitors and language arbiter by focusing on the interpretation of the testimony given by General Hideki Tojo, who had been Prime Minister of Japan for most of the duration of the Pacific War (having taken office on October 18, 1941, and left office on July 18, 1944). The linguistic quality of the interpreting is not covered here, because the limited availability of the soundtrack of Tojo's sessions makes microlinguistic analysis of intonations, hesitations, pauses and other features of actual speech impractical. Instead, the focus here is on how the linguists behaved: how the monitors addressed what they perceived as interpreting problems, what kind of spontaneous remarks, if any, the interpreters made, and how the language arbiter performed his role. The aim is to analyze the linguists' behaviour in connection with their relative positions in the institutional hierarchy and the power relations connected with their different levels of language competence.

There are two main reasons for focusing on the testimony of Hideki Tojo. First, it provides one of the largest sets of samples of interpretations in both directions between Japanese and English, and of monitors' interjections, for any single witness. During the question-and-answer sessions, which were among the longest of all the testimonies given by any of the defendants, each of the three main monitors worked for more than one session. Thus, data is available for comparing the behaviour of different monitors. Tojo's testimony also represents one of the most accessible segments of the films of the proceedings that are stored in the U.S. National Archives. Since their soundtracks are available, the problems arising from relying solely on the transcripts (see Gile 1999) can be mitigated to some degree. Further, focusing on Tojo's testimony permits reference to the work of Tomie Watanabe (1998), which was the first academic inquiry into interpreting at the Tokyo Trial and includes an analysis of the interpreting during Tojo's testimony. Although Watanabe's more language-oriented focus differs from the approach taken in this chapter, some of the data she collected is incorporated in the examination of the linguists' behaviour.

The second reason for focusing on Tojo's testimony is to minimize the variables in the factors that may have affected the behaviour of the linguists. Tojo was one of the last witnesses at the trial and his testimony was given in the twentieth month of the proceedings. Interpreters who had shown conspicuous cognitive limitations, such as late response or memory problems, would have been dismissed by that time. It is also probable that, as Watanabe has suggested (1998, 57), the most competent, knowledgeable and experienced interpreters were assigned to work on his testimony, given that he was considered the most influential figure in Japan's wartime activities and his testimony attracted close attention both in Japan and around the world (see, for example, "Tribunal Packed For Tojo Phase," *Nippon Times*, December 27, 1947).

Monitors and Interpreters during Tojo's Testimony

Tojo first took the witness stand on December 27, 1947, when his defense counsel, George Blewett, started reading out his affidavit and the monitor began a simultaneous reading of the prepared translation. Direct examination by Blewett started on the afternoon of December 30, and then the consecutive interpreting by the Japanese interpreters began. Examinations by other defense lawyers followed, then the cross-examination by Chief Prosecutor Joseph Keenan, which continued from the morning of December 31 to the afternoon of January 6, 1948. After further cross-examination by Sir William Webb on behalf of the judges, Tojo's testimony ended on the morning of January 7, 1948, with Blewett's redirect examination. The focus here is on the nine sessions, spread over the mornings and afternoons of six days, during which questions and answers were interpreted consecutively. Captain Edward Kraft was the language arbiter throughout, while the interpreters and monitors alternated (see Table 5.1). It should be noted that the transcripts do not indicate which of the interpreters was interpreting at any particular point in the proceedings.

EXHIBIT 5.1 HIDEKI TOJO AT THE WITNESS STAND

TABLE 5.1

MONITORS AND INTERPRETERS DURING PART OF THE TESTIMONY OF
HIDEKI TOJO BETWEEN DECEMBER 30, 1947, AND JANUARY 7,
1948

	MONITOR	INTERPRETERS
December 30, afternoon	Sho Onodera	Hideki Masaki, Takashi Oka, Toshiro Henry Shimanouchi
December 31, morning	Sho Onodera	Masahito Iwamoto, Makoto Taji, Toshiro Henry Shimanouchi
January 2, morning	Lanny Miyamoto	Toshiro Henry Shimanouchi, Takashi Oka, Makoto Taji, Masao Yamanaka
January 2, afternoon	David Akira Itami	Toshiro Henry Shimanouchi, Masakazu Eric Shimada, Tomio Mori
January 5, morning	David Akira Itami	Toshiro Henry Shimanouchi, Takashi Oka, Makoto Taji, Tomio Mori
January 5, afternoon	Sho Onodera	Toshiro Henry Shimanouchi, Takashi Oka, Tomio Mori
January 6, morning	David Akira Itami	Toshiro Henry Shimanouchi, Tomio Mori, Makoto Taji, Takashi Oka
January 6, afternoon	Sho Onodera	Takashi Oka, Toshiro Henry Shimanouchi, Tomio Mori, Masakazu Eric Shimada
January 7, morning	Lanny Miyamoto	Toshiro Henry Shimanouchi, Masahito Iwamoto, Tomio Mori, Makoto Taji

Their profiles are discussed in detail in Chapter 3, but it is noteworthy that four of the eight interpreters assigned to these parts of Tojo's testimony were from the Ministry of Foreign Affairs. It should also be noted that the interpreters had relatively privileged backgrounds, as evidenced by their family connections with prominent figures, their education in the United States and at private international schools in Japan, and their experience in diplomatic posts overseas. In contrast, the monitors, as sons of immigrants to the United States, had had to fight prejudice and discrimination in American society.

The Behaviour of the Monitors

According to Tomie Watanabe (1998, 19, 29, 37), during Tojo's testimony the interpreters interpreted 1,178 English utterances into Japanese (131 per session on average) and 845 Japanese utterances into English (94 per session on average), and the number of interjections by the monitors was 161 for interpretation from English into Japanese (18 per session on average) and 35 for interpretation from Japanese into English (four per session on average). This means that the monitor interjected thirteen percent of the times when the interpretation was from English into Japanese and four percent of the times when the interpretation was from Japanese into English. These statistics, however, cover only the interjections recorded in the English and Japanese transcripts. Checking the transcripts against the available soundtracks of the films of the Trial indicates that the transcripts are accurate as far as they go, but do not include those of the monitors' interjections that were whispered to the interpreters. These soundtracks, which are accessible at the U.S. National Archives, represent only about twenty percent of the sessions devoted to Tojo's testimony, so the following examination of the monitors' interjections is focused not on the exact numbers of interjections in certain categories but on the relative frequency of interjections by individuals or by types.

It is a qualitative rather than quantitative analysis of the available data, based on the author's own knowledge and experience as an interpreter and researcher.

The monitors' interjections may be divided into four categories. The first comprises corrections of errors. Different typologies have been used for the analysis of errors in interpreting, and there has been some criticism of the lack of consideration for pragmatic and functional aspects in such analyses (Pöchhacker 2004, 142–43). The errors considered here are those for which the reasons for correction by the monitors can be identified in the transcripts. They are mainly omissions and errors of meaning, including those involving numbers, although a few additions are also found. These three types of errors (omissions, errors of meaning, additions) are more or less in line with the classic typology proposed by Barik (1975/2002). The second category comprises rephrasings, where the monitor offered his own version of an interpretation even though it appears from the transcripts that there was no correctible error. The third category comprises direct interactions with Tojo and other participants in the proceedings. The fourth category brings together the other types of interjection by the monitors, including interruptions of the interpreters to finish interpretations, and whispering instructions that are not reflected in the transcripts.

Although none of the Tribunal's official documents gives a clear definition of the role that the monitors were expected to play, it is presumed that their main function was to correct errors of interpretation. To take an example of a monitor adding information omitted by an interpreter, this is what happened on the morning of January 7, 1948, when Chief Prosecutor Joseph Keenan objected to a question put to Tojo by one of the defense counsel (IMTFE Transcripts, p. 36,831; Japanese transcripts, p.349(4) with the author's translation):

Keenan: Mr. President, I object to that question as being an improper one, a sheer waste of time.

Interpreter: *Tadaima no shitsumon wa dato de nai to iu riyu no moto ni, igi o moshitatemasu.* [I object, based on the reason that the question that has just been asked is not appropriate.]

Monitor [Miyamoto]: *Mattaku jikan no kuhi desu.* [It is a total waste of time.]

This is an example of an interjection that was valid and contributed to the completeness of the transcripts but probably did not affect the proceedings either way, since the interpreter's omission of "waste of time" did not change the general meaning of the passage and Tojo did not have to respond to the statement. In the following example, from the afternoon of January 6, 1948, the monitor's interjection may be considered more significant (IMTFE Transcripts, p. 36,779; Japanese transcripts, p.398(9), with the author's translation):

Keenan: You have told us that the Emperor on repeated occasions made known to you that he was a man of peace and did not want war, is that correct?

Interpreter: ... *Anata wa sude ni hotei ni taishite, Nihon Tenno wa heiwa o ai suru hito de aru to iu koto o maemotte anata-gata ni shirashimete atta to iu koto o moshimashita. Kore wa tadashii desu ne.* [You told the court that the Japanese Emperor had made known to you that he was a man who loved peace. Is this correct?]

Monitor [Onodera]: *Sore o kurikaeshite osshaimashita.* [He said that repeatedly.]

The phrase "on repeated occasions" was an important modifier for the prosecutor, who had been directed by the Allied powers to grant total immunity to the Emperor and tried to depict the Emperor as a pacifist who delegated authority to the militarist advisors (Dower 1999, 459–60; Bix 2000, 610–12). This examination took place amid the efforts of the International Prosecution Section and of Tojo himself, in coordination with General MacArthur's office and the Japanese government, to offset the damaging slip that Tojo had made during his testimony on December 31, 1947. Responding to a question from one of the defense counsel, Tojo had inadvertently implicated the Emperor in Japan's wartime activities by stating that "there is no Japanese subject who would go against the will of His Majesty: more particularly, among high officials of the Japanese government" (IMTFE Transcripts, p. 36,251). The commotion that this remark had created was reported in the *Nippon Times* (January 1, 1948) under the headline "Keenan Grills Tojo on East Asia Sphere and Causes of War":

> "You know the implications from that reply", Sir William Webb said. The courtroom became hushed. Attorney [William] Logan hesitated by the lectern for a moment. Various defense attorneys directed wondering gazes at each other. Finally, Mr. Logan said [that] he had no more questions and then took his seat.

According to Takashi Oka, interviewed by the author nearly sixty years later (in Washington, DC, on December 11, 2005), the aspect of the Tokyo Trial that had made the most lasting impression on him was the laborious effort both Keenan and Tojo made never to expose the Emperor for his part in the Japanese war crimes, and the exchanges between them and the frustrated Webb, who had wanted to see the Emperor indicted. In Oka's view, the tensions between Keenan, Tojo and Webb were obvious to everyone present, including the interpreters in the booth. It cannot now be determined whether Onodera interjected on January 6 merely in order to conduct his routine task of monitoring or because he was aware of the significance of the missing words, but in either case the interjection may have served to remind Tojo of what he was expected to say.

In addition to inserting missing information, the monitors also interjected to strike out information added by the interpreters, albeit infrequently. For example, on the afternoon of December 30, 1947, Onodera corrected an addition made by an interpreter during questioning by William Logan Jr., defense counsel for Marquis Koichi Kido (IMTFE Transcripts, p. 36,510; Japanese transcripts, p.344(20) with the author's translation):

> Logan: Now, is it not true that Marquis Kido was only one of a large number of advisors to the Emperor, considering these Cabinet members and members of the Supreme Command, and that Marquis Kido had no say whatsoever in the final determination of decisions?

> Interpreter: *Kido wa kono Tenno o hosasuru hijo ni tasu no mono no tatta hitori ni suginakatta no de atte, saigo ni tosui ni kansuru kettei ni kanshite wa, nanra no hatsugen ga nakatta to iu no wa jijitsu dewa arimasen deshitaka.* [Isn't it true that Kido was only one of the many people who assisted this Emperor and that in fact he had no say whatsoever in the final decisions related to the Supreme Command?]

> Monitor [Onodera]: *Tosui-ken jiko to iu no wa sakujoshimasu. Donna saigo no kettei ni kanshite mo kettei-ken ga nai to iu no ga jijitsu dewa arimasenka.* [Delete "related to the Supreme Command." Isn't it true that he had no right to make decisions, no authority regarding any final decision?]

There is no phrase corresponding to "*tosui-ken jiko*" ("matters related to the Supreme Command") in Logan's question, so Onodera's intervention is understandable. Since the question was directed at Tojo, his answer might well have been different if the addition of this phrase had been left uncorrected. Onodera's intervention thus helped avoid a possible misunderstanding or confusion.

The monitors also corrected a number of other errors, ranging from simple mistakes in interpreting numbers to gross errors of meaning. There were cases in which an interpreter's error was such that the main message of a statement as a whole was changed. For example, the interpretation of Webb's remarks in response to defense counsel's objections on the morning of January 2, 1948, gave them a meaning that was the exact opposite of the original (IMTFE Transcripts, p. 36,572; Japanese transcripts, p.346(3)–(4), with the author's translation):

> President: He was not asked any question that bore on guilt or innocence. He was merely asked his opinion on the law. If I am asked whether I think aggressive war is a crime and I say that I think it is not a crime, am I guilty of anything?

> Interpreter: *Shonin wa yuzai ka mujitsu ka to iu koto ni taishite nanra shitsumon o ukete orimasen. Shonin wa tan ni horitsu no kaishaku ni tsuite shitsumon o uketani sugimasen. Moshi watashi ga shinryaku senso wa hanzai de aruka inaika to iu mondai ni tsuite kikareta baai ni hanzai nari to kotaeta nara watashi wa soko de yuzai ni narimasuka.* [The witness has not been asked any questions about being guilty or innocent. The witness was only asked a question about the interpretation of the law. If I am asked whether or not aggressive war is a crime and I answer that it *is* a crime, will I be found guilty?)

> Monitor [Miyamoto]: *Shinryaku senso wa hanzai de nai to watashi wa kotaeta to sureba, watashi wa tsumi o okashia koto ni narimasuka.* [If I answer that aggressive war is *not* a crime, will it mean that I committed a crime?]

Since Webb's remarks formed part of an exchange with the defense counsel and Keenan and were not directed at Tojo, the interpreting error probably would not have affected the proceedings. However, the error in the next example could have induced a different answer from the witness without the monitor's correction. This exchange took place on the afternoon of January 2, 1948 (IMTFE Transcripts, p. 36,614; Japanese transcripts, p.346(10), with the author's translation):

> Keenan: Well, the Emperor thought this procedure very strange, didn't he? And he said so to Kido.

Interpreter: *Shikashi, kono tetsuzuki, kono yarikata wa domo hijo ni hen da to iu fu ni Tenno wa kangaeta no dewa arimasenka. Soshite Kido mo mata so iu fu ni kangaeta no dewa arimasenka.* [However, didn't the Emperor think that this procedure, this way of doing things, seemed very strange? And didn't Kido think that way as well?]

Monitor [Itami]: *Tenno wa so kangae Kido ni so itta no dewa arimasenka.* [Didn't the Emperor think so *and* say so to Kido?]

All the examples above are valid corrections made on grounds that can be easily recognized in the transcripts of the interpretations. During Tojo's testimony, the number of such corrections was about five to six per session on average (the interpreters interpreted a total of 225 utterances per session on average). About ninety-four percent of those corrections concerned interpretations from English into Japanese. (Possible reasons for this phenomenon are discussed below.) There were a few cases, however, in which a monitor erred in his attempted correction, or did not catch an error made by an interpreter, as in this example, from the morning of January 2, 1948 (IMTFE Transcripts, p. 36,582; Japanese transcripts, p.346(5), with the author's translation):

Keenan: Well, wouldn't you say the plain truth of the matter was that the Yonai Cabinet did not seize the opportunity of making the best of the situation for Japan in its plan for expansion and taking advantage of the turn of events in the European War? Isn't that a rather fair summation of the situation?

Interpreter: *Shikashi, jujitsu o sekirara ni ieba kekkyoku Yonai naikaku wa toji no jokyo o toraete sore no kikai o riyo shite toji no zenbu no josei o riyo shite Nihon no kakucho o hakaru koto, soshite Yoroppa no josei ni umaku binjo suru koto o shinakatta to iu no ga genin de atta to iu no ga jijitsu dewa arimasenka.* [However, if the bare truth is told, wouldn't it be true that it was because the Yonai cabinet did not seize the situation of that time to make use of the opportunity, and make use of the overall situation of that time to seek Japan's expansion, and did not take advantage of the developments in Europe?]

Monitor [Miyamoto]: *Chotto shusei itashimasu. Yonai naikaku wa toji no Oshu Senso no tenkanki o riyo shi, Nihon no kakucho kakudai o suru tame ni sono jiki o riyo shi, kokeiki o riyo shinakatta to iu jotai o tadashiku itta koto ni narimasenka.* [Let me modify it a little. Wouldn't it be correctly referring to the situation that the Yonai cabinet made use of the turning point in the European War at that time and made use of that time for Japan's expansion and enlargement, and didn't make use of the good opportunity?]

Miyamoto's interjection is not in fact intelligible in Japanese. In addition, he erroneously corrected *"josei"* (the developments or situations) to *"tenkanki"* (the turning point) for the Japanese translation of "the turn of events." However, these errors appear not to have caused Tojo any confusion. His response was that "that view is one-sided" and the proceedings moved on. It should also be noted that Miyamoto started with a self-referential comment ("Let me modify it a little") before presenting his version of the interpretation.

During the same session, Miyamoto failed to correct some errors and Keenan, prompted by a Japanese-speaking colleague, corrected them instead (IMTFE Transcripts, p. 36,563; Japanese transcripts, p.346(2), with the author's translation):

Keenan: Now, lastly, and not at all unimportant, is the third item of losses of the Imperial Army, including the Nomonhan Incident, killed, 109,250 Japanese.

Interpreter: *Sara ni kore wa juyo na mondai dewa nai keredomo, kono shita ni sara ni suji ga arawarete orimasu. Sore wa Nomonhan ni okeru mono o fukumu tokoro no Nihon-gun no songai to natte orimashite 19,250 to arawarete orimasu.* [In addition, although this is not an important issue, there is another number that appears below this. It states that it is the losses the Japanese Army suffered, including those at Nomonhan, and it says 19,250.]

Tojo: *Sore wa itsu no koto desu*. [What point in time are you referring to?]

Keenan: Just a moment. My colleague, Mr. Maxon, who speaks the Japanese language, calls my attention to the fact that the translation was "not important." I said, "not *un*important," and I wish it was translated.

Interpreter: *Tadaima watashi no doryo de arimasu Nihongo o hanasu kensatsukan no chukoku ni yoreba, watashi wa juyo de aru to itta no o juyo de nai to iu guai ni yakusarete iru so desu. Teisei shite kudasai.* [According to advice from my colleague, a Japanese-speaking prosecutor, it appears that the part where I said "important" was translated as "unimportant." Please make a correction.]

Tojo: *Teisei, wakarimashita ga, hajime kara itte kudasai. Kekkyoku nani o otazune ni naru no desuka.* [The correction is noted. Please state it from the beginning. What do you want to ask after all?]

Interpreter: I understand the correction, but may I have the whole question repeated? What are you asking me?

These examples of erroneous corrections and uncorrected errors indicate that the monitors were not always reliable checkers of the accuracy of interpretation. (The interpreters' reactions to the monitor's erroneous corrections are discussed below.)

In addition to correcting errors found in the interpretations, the monitors sometimes presented their own versions, rewording and changing sentence structures and adding information, after the interpreters had given versions that appear to have been free of errors. During Tojo's testimony such rephrasings occurred about nine times per session on average, and about ninety-four percent of them concerned interpretation from English into Japanese. In many of these cases, the interpreter's version as recorded in the transcripts does not seem to warrant an intervention by the monitor and the monitor's version does not seem to show any improvement. For example, the interpretation of a question put by Keenan on the morning of January 2, 1948, has no addition or omission and delivers the original meaning coherently, yet Miyamoto interjected anyway (IMTFE Transcripts, p. 36,560; Japanese transcripts, p.346(2), with the author's translation):

> Keenan: And the next entry is "The Booty"; and it includes "Arms, 482,257." Wouldn't that indicate that that was attempting to get an exact figure?

> Interpreter: *Sono tsugi no kisaijiko wa senrihin to natte orimasu. Soshite buki to iu kou ni 482,257 to kaite arimasu. Kore o mite mo hijo ni seikaku na suji o arawasu to shite iru fu ni natte orimasenka.* [The next entry is "The Booty." And it states 482,257 under the item "Arms." Looking at this, doesn't it appear to be trying to present a very accurate number?]

> Monitor [Miyamoto]: *Seikaku na suji o motomeyo to doryoku shite iru to iu koto ga ukagawaremasenka, sore ni yotte.* [According to that, can't you sense that it is making efforts to seek an exact number?]

On the morning of January 2, 1948, Miyamoto seems to have been attempting to clarify a question in order to help Tojo understand it (IMTFE Transcripts, p. 36,589; Japanese transcripts, p.346(7), with the author's translation):

> Keenan: I withdraw that question for the moment, and ask you this: do you recall that the United States entered into the World War in 1917?

> Tojo (through Interpreter): Yes, very well.

> Keenan: That didn't cause any convulsion in Japan, did it?

Interpreter: *Sore ga tame ni Nihon ni oite doran ga shojita to iu koto wa nakatta no dewa arimasenka.* [That didn't cause a convulsion in Japan, did it?]

Monitor [Miyamoto]: *Beikoku ga sekai-sen ni sansen shita koto ni yotte, Nihon ni eikyo o oyobo shita koto wa arimasen desho.* [The entry of the United States into the World War did not affect Japan, did it?]

In another case, on the afternoon of January 6, 1948, Onodera interjected to add information in order to make the implication of an analogy explicit (IMTFE Transcripts: 36,793–36,794; Japanese transcripts, p.348(11), with the author's translation):

Tojo (through Interpreter): I shall reply to that question from two directions. The first, the effect of the Nine-Power Treaty on Japan is something like this: A ten-year old child having been given clothes to fit its age, now having reached the age of eighteen years finds that the clothes are becoming somewhat torn. Japan was trying and trying to mend those tears, but since her body had grown that was impossible.

Keenan: Well, I suggest to you that there was a possibility of sticking a pin in now and then in the process of mending the dress. Would you accept that revision?

Interpreter: *Shikashi kimono o shuzen suru baai ni wa, tokidoki hari o sasu to iu koto mo arimasu. So iu koto o anata wa mitomemasuka.* [However, when a kimono is being mended, sometimes sticking in a pin happens. Would you accept such a thing?]

Monitor [Onodera]: *Sunawachi hari o sasu to moshimasu no wa sono tokidoki ni atatte kaizen subeki wa kaizenshi aratamubeki koto wa aratameru to iu koto o anata wa mitomemasuka.* [In other words, as to the reference to sticking in a pin, would you accept that at appropriate times improvement is made to what should be improved and correction is made to what should be corrected?]

Tojo (through Interpreter): That is perfectly true, but the body grew too quickly for that, and the child's parents wouldn't mend those tears for her.

It cannot be determined whether Onodera's intervention facilitated Tojo's understanding of Keenan's question, but in his answer Tojo kept to the analogical framework that he had initiated and Keenan had adopted, so it is clear that it did not cause any confusion.

In the instances cited so far, the monitors' interjections probably helped Tojo understand the questions put to him. However, the explanation added by Itami in the following example, on the morning of January 6, 1948, seems to go beyond mere clarification (IMTFE Transcripts, p. 36,754; Japanese transcripts, p.348(5), with the author's translation):

> Keenan: Was this principle of making the population of China contribute to the preparation for war with Soviet Russia based on the experience derived by the Kwantung Army from using the population of Manchuria for the same purpose?

> Interpreter: *Tadaima no shisakuyoryo no naka ni kaite arimasu tokoro no genjumin o taisosen junbi ni shiseshimeru to iu koto wa Kanto-gun ni oite genjumin o sono mae ni taisosen junbi wa tsukatta keiken kara kite orunodesuka.* [Did the idea of using local people for the preparation for war against the Soviets, which is written in the "General Outline of Administration," come from the Kwantung Army's prior experience of using local people for preparation for war against the Soviets?]

> Monitor [Itami]: *Ima no tokoro o setsumei shimasu. Hokushi ni chuoseifu o kensetsu seshimete Hokushi no genjumin o taisosen junbi ni shiseshimeru to iu koto wa Kanto-gun wa katte Manshu ni oite Manshu no genjumin o so iu senso junbi ni shiseshimeta keiken ni motozuita tokoro kara deta mono de arimasuka.* [Let me explain this point. Did the idea of establishing a central government in northern China and using the local people of northern China

for the preparation for war against the Soviets come from the experience that the Kwantung Army in Manchuria once used the local people in Manchuria for the preparation for such a war?]

In this case, Keenan's line of questioning concerned a document called the "General Outline of Administration," and the interpreter made Keenan's term "the principle" more explicit by specifying that it was a principle referred to in this document. This would have been sufficient for Tojo to understand the question, but Itami added still more information by explaining the contents of the document, an addition that seems totally unwarranted. It should also be noted that Itami started with a self-referential remark to indicate that he was going to provide an explanation of the question to Tojo.

There were also cases in which a monitor's attempt to make something more explicit confused the witness. On the morning of December 31, 1947, for example, Tojo's response to information added by Onodera resulted in the discourse taking a direction different from that of the original questioning (IMTFE Transcripts, pp. 36,538–36,539; Japanese transcripts, p.345(5), with the author's translation):

Keenan: You advocated the process of peace terms being arranged between China and Japan in 1941 while there was a huge Japanese army occupying a large part of China, is that not correct?

Interpreter: *Shina no hijo ni hiroi chiiki o bakudai na kazu no Nihon-gun ga senryo shitsutsu aru aida ni* ... [While an enormous number of Japanese troops were in the process of occupying a very large area in China—

Monitor [Onodera]: —*aida ni, anata wa 1941-nen Nisshi-kan no wahei no joken o teiji shita no dewa arimasenka.* [—during that time, didn't you present peace terms between Japan and China in 1941?]

Tojo: *Motto hakkiri itte kudasai.* [Please state it more clearly.]

Interpreter: May I have that question repeated? It was not quite comprehensible.

Keenan: Will you please answer that question directly without making a speech?

[no interpretation]

Monitor [Onodera]: We are trying to get an accurate translation on this last one. We have not done so yet.

Tojo: *Ima no ron, mo sukoshi hakkiri itte kudasai.* [On this current matter, please state it a little more clearly.]

Monitor [Onodera]: *Shina no kodai na chiiki ni Nihon no taigun ga chuzai shite oru toki ni oite, anata wa Shina to Nihon to no aida no heiwa joken, wahei kosho nado to iu koto o tsuzukete otta no dewa arimasenka. So iu mujun shita jotai ni oite—* [While a large Japanese army was stationed in a large area in China, weren't you continuing to have peace terms between China and Japan, peace negotiations or something? In such a contradictory situation—

Tojo: *Hitotsu mo mujun shite orimasen ga, tozen tsuzukemashita.* [It is not contradictory at all, naturally I continued.]

Interpreter: There is no inconsistency in the situation. I naturally continued such efforts for peace.

In an effort to help Tojo to understand Keenan's question, Onodera added the term "*mujun shita*" (contradictory), which is rather forceful language in Japanese. Because of this addition, Tojo ended up responding directly to the forcefulness of the phrase, instead of responding to a valid interpretation of Keenan's original question.

During Tojo's testimony, the monitors occasionally interacted with Tojo directly by explaining procedural and translation issues to him, asking him for clarifications and responding to his questions. There were two to three such instances in each of the sessions under examination here. For example, during examination by defense counsel on December 30, 1947, Onodera clarified with the witness the portion that had been explicated by the interpreter in order to see if the interpreter's choice was correct (IMTFE Transcripts, p. 36,503; Japanese transcripts, p.344(18), with the author's translation):

Tojo: *Watashi no seikaku to shite mata watashi no hoshin to shite juyo naru tokoro no gaiko ni tsukimashite wa kore wa togai sekininsha, sunawachi Gaimu Daijin to sodan shimasu. Gunji ni kanshite wa kare ni wa issai yokai sasemasen.* [Both by nature and as my policy, on important foreign affairs I consult the person responsible, that is, the Foreign Minister. As for military affairs, I do not allow him to interfere at all.]

Interpreter: Both by my nature and as a matter of policy, on all important matters concerning foreign affairs I consulted that Foreign Minister; and as for military affairs, I did not allow Hoshino to interfere.

Monitor [Onodera]: *Kare ni wa yokai sasemasen to iu no wa Gaimu Daijin no koto desuka.* [When you say "I do not allow him to interfere," are you referring to the Foreign Minister?]

Tojo: *Hoshino no koto desu.* [I am referring to Hoshino.]

The monitors sometimes offered the witness explanations on the procedural and translation issues that concerned him. In particular, the monitor interjected to guide Tojo to the appropriate page or paragraph in a document when there were discrepancies in the numbering of pages and paragraphs, between the exhibit in Japanese that the witness was given and the English translation used to ask questions. There were also instances of confusion when the witness was handed an original Japanese document as an exhibit and a questioner referred to a word or phrase mistranslated by the translator in the English version of the document. The following exchange took place during the afternoon of January 2, 1948 (IMTFE Transcripts, pp. 36,609–36,610; Japanese transcripts, p.346(10), with the author's translation):

Keenan: Well, to simplify the matter, Mr. Tojo, and to come back to [Marquis] Kido['s] diary, I will quote his language. He said that the War Minister had just secretly recommended Tojo for War Minister, and I suggest to you that that was the language of Kido and not my own. Do you say [that] Kido was wrong about that?

Interpreter: *Sore dewa mondai o kantan ni suru tame ni watashi wa futatabi Kido nikki ni modori sono naiyo kara inyo shimasu. Kare wa sono naka de Rikuso yori konin ni Tojo o naiso—* [Then, to simplify the matter, I am going back to Kido's diary again and quoting from its contents. In it he says that the War Minister unofficially recommended Tojo as his successor to the Emperor by *naiso*—]

Monitor [Itami]: *Sore wa Nihon-bun no genbun ni wa naiso to arimasu ga, kensatsukan no yomareta eibun ni wa himitsuri ni Tenno ni suisen shita aruiwa suisen shita to iu kotoba ga arimasu.* [Here, the original text in Japanese says "*naiso*," but the English text that the prosecutor read out says "secretly recommended to the Emperor" or "recommended to the throne."]

Tojo: *Sore wa naiso-suru to iu kotoba o honyaku ga machigatte oru no desu. Naiso to iu koto wa himitsu de mo nandemo nai no desu. Sore de Nihon no naiso to iu koto ga nakanaka owakari ni naranu kara, watashi wa sakihodo yoku setsumei shiyo to omotte oshikari o uketa no desu.* [The translation of the phrase "*naiso suru*" is mistaken. "*Naiso*" is not "secret" at all. Since you do not fully understand "*naiso*" in Japan, I was going to explain it well, and got scolded.]

Interpreter: In the first place, the translation is mistaken with regard to the word "*naiso*"—informal recommendation. There is nothing secret about "*naiso*." It was because you did not appear to understand what I meant by "*naiso*," informal recommendation, that I tried to repeat my explanation to you and received the reprimand of the Court.

"*Naiso*" means "an unofficial report," specifically from a subject to the Emperor. Keenan used an improper translation for "*naiso*"— "secret recommendation". If Itami had not intervened, Tojo might have continued answering the question without knowing that there had been an error.

Providing such explanations to Tojo probably helped him and the court avoid possible confusion arising from procedural or interpreting issues. However, once again, an interjection by Itami on the morning of January 6, 1948, seems to have gone beyond clarification (IMTFE Transcripts, p. 36,740; Japanese transcripts, p.348(3), with the author's translation):

Keenan: But you still insist that when the Foreign Minister of Japan at that critical moment was sending a message to his own ambassador that he was employing diplomatic language that had various meanings and not using a direct instruction?

Interpreter: *Sore de anata wa nao kono judai naru jiki ni oite Nihon no Gaimu Daijin ga sono taishi ni taishite tsushin o okuru toki ni, iroiro na imi ni torero tokoro no gaikoteki jirei o mochiite ori, soshite chokusai naru kunrei o hasshite oranakatta to iu koto o shucho nasaru no desuka.* [Then, do you still assert that at the critical time the Foreign Minister of Japan sent his ambassador a communication that used diplomatic language that could be interpreted in various ways and did not convey a direct instruction?]

Monitor [Itami]: *Chotto sono ten o setsumei shimasu. Shonin, gokai no nai yo ni. Kono kunrei no naka ni tsukatte aru kotoba wa gaikojo no kotoba de aruka doka, soretomo sono tori no koto o imi shite orunoka to iu imi no shitsumon de arimasu.* [Let me explain this point a little. Mr. Witness, please do not misunderstand. This question means to ask whether the language included in the instruction is diplomatic language or means what it says.]

Tojo: *Sono kotoba no tori desu. Shikashi, seiji to iu mono wa shinde wa orimasen. 8000-man doho no ue ni tatte oru tokoro no seiji to iu mono wa ikite orimasu.* [It means what the language says. But politics has not died. Politics standing on eighty million fellow countrymen is still alive.]

Interpreter: The words meant what they said. But politics isn't a dead thing. It is a living force standing on our 80 million people.

The interpretation does not seem to have been unclear, but Itami intervened to explain the intention of the question. He even warned Tojo not to get confused. It cannot be determined whether Itami's explanation actually helped Tojo or gave him time to prepare his answer carefully. It should be noted that in this instance, once again, Tojo responded directly to the language that Itami used, and not to the language in Keenan's original question.

The monitors also interrupted Tojo and told him to break down his answers for the interpreter. Although these instances are not indicated in the transcripts, Miyamoto's blunt interruption, "*Chotto matte* [Wait a second]" can be heard frequently on the soundtrack. As far as the transcripts and the available soundtrack are concerned, there is nothing to indicate that the monitors interrupted counsel, since a flashing light was available to remind them to break down their questions into interpretable segments. It may be that the monitors had to interrupt Tojo because he did not pay attention to the light. However, the monitors may also have felt less inhibited about interrupting Tojo than they would have about interrupting counsel.

In addition to interacting with the witness, the monitor communicated to the court on behalf of the interpreter to explain interpreting issues and directly respond to the court's questions about interpreting. The monitor also requested, on behalf of the interpreter, that the Japanese and/or English court reporters read aloud their records when the interpreter had trouble recalling a speaker's remarks or when clarification was needed before an interpretation was made.

At times, interpreters seem to have spontaneously made corrections of their own work, although all the self-corrections in the available portions of the soundtrack of Tojo's testimony were prompted by whispered interjections by a monitor. There were also instances in which a monitor interrupted an interpreter and finished the interpretation in his place, as on the morning of January 7, 1948 (IMTFE Transcripts, p. 36,832; Japanese transcripts, p.349(4), with the author's translation):

Defense Counsel [George Blewett]: Sir, there is a clear intimation in the Chief Prosecutor's question as to these five men being dominant in Manchuria, and certainly an intimation and an inference that they assisted him or put him in this position or some nefarious reasons.

Interpreter: *Shikashi, kensatsugawa wa kare no kensatsukan no hantai-jinmon no sai ni oite, korera no gomei no otoko ga Manshu ni oite saiko no seiryoku o shimete oru jinbutsu de aru. Nanika no riyu ni yotte korera no otoko ga sono hikoku o sono chii ni oshiageru koto wo—* [However, in the cross-examination by the prosecutor, the prosecution side [words missing] these five men were the people who had the greatest influence in Manchuria. For some reason, these men pushed this defendant into that position—

Monitor [Miyamoto]: *Kono gonin no otoko wa Manshu ni oite hijo ni haburi o furutta mono de ari, akuratsu na riyu no moto ni, kono Tojo wo jikan ni osubeku enjoshita. Ko gengai ni fukumete sono koto o itte orimasu.* [These five men were people who greatly exercised their influence, and for nefarious reasons they assisted with the intention of recommending this [man] Tojo to the Vice Minister. That is what has been said with this implication.]

In fact, Miyamoto interrupted the interpreters on more than a few occasions, but since the soundtrack for these portions is not available it cannot be determined if this was because the interpreter was struggling, because Miyamoto was impatient, or for other reasons. Nevertheless, it is clear from the transcripts of Tojo's testimony that Miyamoto frequently interjected to rephrase English-to-Japanese interpretations and to finish off such interpretations as well. This pattern of behaviour seems to reflect Miyamoto's approach to his task, rather than any unusual incompetence on the part of the interpreters. Miyamoto almost never interjected after interpretations from Japanese into English, and he had fewer interactions with Tojo and other participants than the other monitors did.

Itami was very active in all four of the categories of interjection (set out above) and in both language directions (English to Japanese and Japanese to English). He was also very active in explaining interpreting and procedural issues to the court. However, he rephrased interpretations less frequently than the other monitors.

Finally, there was nothing conspicuous in Onodera's behaviour as compared to that of the other two monitors. He made quite a few valid corrections, but he did not provide seemingly unwarranted explanations as often as Itami did, nor did he interrupt interpreters in order to complete their interpretations as frequently as Miyamoto did.

The Behaviour of the Interpreters

According to both Takashi Oka (2005, interview with the author) and Masakazu Shimada (2000), in principle, the interpreters were not expected to speak on their own behalf in open court. On occasion, however, they responded directly to questions by the witness and the court, and they sometimes spontaneously provided explanations to witnesses on procedural matters. Although there were only about a dozen such interjections during the nine sessions being examined here, they are all of some interest for the light they shed on the interpreters' attitudes and behaviour.

On several occasions, an interpreter, rather than a monitor, provided a quick and direct response to a request from Tojo for clarification, as, for example, on the morning of December 31, 1947 (IMTFE Transcripts, p. 36,550; Japanese transcripts, p.345(9), with the author's translation):

> Keenan: We will pass to another subject for a moment. Did the United States have anything to do with Japan embarking upon its career in Manchuria in 1931?
>
> Interpreter: *1931-nen Nihon ga Manshu ni okeru kodo o kaishi suru ni atatte Beikoku wa nanika sore ni kankei arimashitaka.* [Did the United States have anything to do with Japan embarking upon its activity in Manchuria in 1931?]
>
> Tojo: *Eikoku desuka, Beikoku desuka.* [The United Kingdom or the United States?]
>
> Interpreter: *Beikoku, Amerika.* [The United States, America.]

On the morning of January 6, 1948, Keenan asked if he had missed an interpretation and the interpreter responded without first interpreting Keenan's remarks into Japanese (IMTFE Transcripts, p. 36,737):

> Keenan: Was there something said by the witness that I didn't get the translation of? Perhaps the Court did.
>
> Interpreter: The witness asked if another question had been asked.

In these instances, the interpreters were perhaps reacting instinctively or did not feel the need to defer to the monitor because they were dealing with simple questions that could be resolved with only a few words. There is nothing in the transcripts to suggest that the court or the monitors disapproved when the interpreters took what might have been seen as liberties in this way.

On other occasions, when an interpreter was interrupted and missed an opportunity to interpret an answer by Tojo in its entirety, the interpreter inserted the omitted part just after the interruption, as on the afternoon of January 2, 1948 (IMTFE Transcripts, p. 36,605; Japanese transcripts, p.346(9), with the author's translation):

> Keenan: I am suggesting to you, Mr. Tojo, that it would be possible for things to be happening in Tokyo that you knew about and helped to plan without your being there. You will agree that was a possibility, will you not?

> Interpreter: *Shikashi hitotsu no kanosei no mondai de arimasu ga, anata ga Tokyo ni inakute mo Tokyo de okotte oru koto ni tsuite anata ga shitteta to iu koto wa oi ni ariuru koto da to iu koto o kiite oru no de arimasu ga, so dewa arimasenka.* [But, as a matter of possibility, isn't it true that it is quite possible that you knew what was happening in Tokyo, even if you were not in Tokyo?]

> Tojo: *Watashi ni wa sozo dekimasen.* [I cannot imagine that.]

> Monitor [Itami]: *Anata ga shitte oru koto de ari, soshite anata ga ritsuan moshiku wa keikaku no sokushin o enjo shita to iu yo na dekigoto ni tsuite shitte orieta de aro to iu no ga shitsumon de arimasu.* [The question was about whether you could know it, you could know about the matters you planned or helped in promoting the plan.]

> Tojo: *Oriemasen. Oriemasen to iukoto wa ima watashi ga itta tori.* [It is not possible. It is not possible, as I have just said.]

> Interpreter: Just prior to the Japanese rendition, the witness said, "I cannot imagine." His last reply was, "I could not have known."

The interpreters' desire to render everything the witness said is apparent in the following example, from the morning of January 2, 1948 (IMTFE Transcripts, p. 36,566; Japanese transcripts, p.346(3), with the author's translation):

Tojo: *Sore wa sono tori. Tadashi*— [That's right, but—]

Interpreter: Yes, as you say, but—

Keenan: You finally, in your affidavit, have referred to it as a war, have you not?

Interpreter: Before Mr. Prosecutor's question was put, the witness was just about to state his next answer.

Keenan: I question that, Language Section, or whoever is making that statement, but if the witness wishes to make some other statement, I do not wish to cut him off. I am looking at him.

Since the interpreters were not supposed to speak on their own behalf, there were very few interjections of this type. In fact, after this instance, the interpreters never again interrupted the speaker during Tojo's testimony.

On a few occasions, however, an interpreter offered Tojo an explanation of a procedural matter, as in this instance from the morning of January 2, 1948 (IMTFE Transcripts, p. 36,595; Japanese transcripts, with the author's translation):

Keenan: Now, I will ask you to refer to that document, Exhibit 541—you have it there with you—"1. Basic Policy." Will you look at that; and I want to call your particular attention to the second sentence. Have you read it?

Interpreter: *Dewa, anata no temoto ni aru sono shorui o mite kudasai. Soko ni 1. Konpon Hoshin to iu no ga arimasu. Soshite dai-ni banme no bunsho o toku ni chui shite mite kudasai.—Eigo no ni banme no bunsho desu kara atehamaranai kamo shiremasen. Yomimashitaka.* [Now, please look at the document you have there. It is "1. Basic

Policy" there. And please pay particular attention to the second passage.—It is the second passage in English, so it may not be relevant.—Did you read it?)

Tojo: *Yonde imasu yo.* [I am reading it.]

Interpreter: Yes, I am reading it. All right.

Keenan: Does it not say, as to basic policy, and I quote: "First of all, it is directed toward the construction of a new order of Greater East Asia built upon a firm solidarity of Japan, Manchukuo and China, with this Empire as the centre"?

Interpreter: *Ko iu fu ni kaite arimasenka. "Mazu kokoku o kakushin to shi Nichi-Man-Shi no kyoko naru ketsugo o konpon to suru Daitoa no shin-chitsujo o kensetsu suru ni ari"?* [Doesn't it say, "First of all, it is directed toward the construction of a new order of Greater East Asia built upon a firm solidarity of Japan, Manchukuo and China with this Empire as the centre"?]

Tojo: *Sore wa arimasu. Chotto matte kudasai. Sore wa tashika ni arimashita.* [It is there. Please wait a moment. It was certainly there.]

Interpreter: Yes—will you wait just a moment? *Nihon-bun no 1-peji desu. 1. kihon-hoshin no naka desu.* [It's the first page of the Japanese text. It's in "1. Basic Policy".]

Tojo: *Arimashita.* [There it was.]

Interpreter: Yes, I have found it.

This type of assistance was usually offered by Itami and Onodera when they were acting as monitor, but when Miyamoto was monitoring the interpreters seem to have stepped in on their own initiative.

As has been discussed above, during Tojo's testimony there were several instances in which a monitor rephrased seemingly error-free interpretations or corrected interpretations erroneously. The transcripts and the available film soundtracks indicate that the interpreters never objected to or indicated any difference from these interjections, with just one exception when Miyamoto repeated the same erroneous correction (described on p.102), which occurred on the morning of January 2, 1948 (IMTFE Transcripts, p. 36,592; Japanese transcripts p.346(7), with the author's translation):

> Keenan: Well, the point of the question is that we are talking about the world being on the threshold of a stupendous historic change that affected the policy of Japan. Now, one of the reasons you have ascribed was the turn of events that took place in the European War. And you further stated, Mr. Tojo, that the fall of France about the 17ᵗʰ of June, 1940—

> Interpreter: *Wareware ga ima hanashite iru koto wa, sunawachi sekai wa Nihon no kokusaku ni eikyo o oyoboshita tokoro no rekishiteki ichidaitenki ni hochaku shite iru to iu koto de arimashite, sono riyu no hitotsu to shite*— [What we are discussing now is that the world was facing a historical, a big turning point, which affected the national policy of Japan, and one of the reasons was—]

> Monitor [Miyamoto]: *Oshu ni okeru tenkanki o riyu no hitotsu to shite anata wa agete orimasu.* [You cite the turning point in Europe as one of the reasons.]

> Interpreter: *Oshu no josei no suii*— [The developments in the situation in Europe—]

In summary, the interpreters' interjections were mainly intended to help Tojo to understand the questions being put to him and the procedural matters that concerned him, and to guide him to the appropriate pages and passages in documents introduced as exhibits. They also interrupted the proceedings to ensure that Tojo was able to complete his answers, and were diligent about providing full interpretations of his testimony. Whenever the interpreter missed an opportunity to interpret a part of a statement by Tojo, he tried to insert the missing part as soon as possible after the interruption.

The Language Arbiter in Action

The transcripts of Tojo's testimony show that the language arbiter, Captain Edward Kraft, spoke on five language issues. Only one of them was addressed at the time the issue arose, and the other four were addressed four to sixteen days after the issues had been referred to the Language Arbitration Board. For example, on December 30, 1947, one of the defense counsel drew attention to a misleading translation of the Japanese word "*joshu*" as "right-hand man" when it should have been translated as "assistant" (IMTFE Transcripts, p. 36,499). It was not until the beginning of the afternoon of January 5, 1948, that Kraft announced the correction to "assistant" approved by the Language Arbitration Board (IMTFE Transcripts, p. 36,683).

During the morning of January 6, 1948, there were some exchanges concerning how "*hantai-teian*" or "*taian*" should be translated, but Kraft could not provide a ruling on the spot. As Tojo pointed out, the original Japanese text of one of the exhibits contained the word "*taian*," which should have been translated as "response," but the translators on the prosecution side had translated it as "counterproposal," and it had then been back-translated as "*hantai-teian*" in the Japanese version of the exhibit as submitted to the court. When one of the interpreters used "*hantai-teian*" instead of the original word "*taian*" in an interpretation, Tojo became confused and complained that there had been a mistranslation. Kraft, who seems not to have understood what the issue was, suggested changing "counterproposal" to "opposing proposal" (a more literal translation of *hantai-teian*), but did not address Tojo's concern.

Without clear agreement having been reached among the parties, Keenan moved on to another question (IMTFE Transcripts, pp. 36,731–36,732).

The only dispute Kraft was able to address on the spot concerned the Japanese word "*fumei*". On January 6, 1948, when asked about his alliance with Pu-Yi, who eventually "betrayed" him, Tojo answered, "*Watashi no fumei de arimasho.*" This was interpreted as "it must have been my lack of virtue," and defense counsel George Blewett objected (IMTFE Transcripts, p. 36,779):

> Defense Counsel [Blewett]: If the Tribunal please, may I have that answer which refers to "lack of virtue" referred to the Language Section? I am informed by my associate counsel that it is not perfectly clear.
>
> Keenan: I am suggesting to the President that it is not worthwhile to take the time of this court, but I suppose we will have to follow the ordinary rule.
>
> President: It is referred accordingly. Captain Kraft.
>
> Language Arbiter: The word in question is "*fumei*," translated, "lack of insight."

There is nothing in the transcripts to indicate how Kraft came up with "lack of insight" on the spot. It would be unrealistic to infer that Kraft, who had had only one year of Japanese training, came up with a translation of this classical, literary word by himself, so presumably there was a brief discussion among the Language Section personnel present in the courtroom. According to Masakazu Shimada (2000, 33), it was the interpreter Toshiro Henry Shimanouchi who interjected to add "virtue and insight" after the original interpretation was made, although this is not reflected in the transcripts.

Interpreting and Power Relations

The interpreters were at the bottom of the hierarchy in the Language Section of the IMTFE, being under the supervision of the section chief, the language arbiter and the monitors. Given the fact that the interpreters were citizens of an occupied country, they presumably were not in a position to have a voice in how the trial proceedings operated. Based on the above examination of their behaviour during Tojo's testimony, it appears that they acted in accordance with their standing within the institutional and political power constellations of the Tribunal. In particular, they spoke on their own behalf only on very infrequent occasions, and they did not object to any of the monitors' interventions, even when they may well have seemed unnecessary or erroneous.

Although Masakazu Shimada admits (2000, 34) that there were "joint efforts," in the sense that the monitors helped by taking notes of numbers and so on, he claims that the interpreters were much more competent than the monitors; that the monitors, apart from David Akira Itami, were not competent enough to correct interpreting errors and that the monitors actually depended on the interpreters (Shimada 2000, 21 and 23). Even so, it is likely that the interpreters felt they were not in any position to protest against or complain about any undue interjections by the monitors. Shimada compares the relations between the interpreters and the monitors to those between a racehorse and a jockey (2000, 23 and 25)(the author's translation):

> For the monitors, the interpreters were like horses ... They
> thought that they were like jockeys. So, for example, someone
> would be speaking, say, a witness speaking, a prosecutor speaking,
> and [the monitor] observed a pause between sentences and pushed
> the switch at the end of an appropriate chunk [of the speech] ...
> Then the red lamp went on at the witness stand.... As for who got

assigned, you know, we were like racehorses, so Mr. Itami would consult the other monitors and say, "Shimada, you go there," and assign [the interpreters] to the seats.

Shimada may be implying that the horse (the interpreter) had to keep running regardless of the competence of the jockey (the monitor) and could not stop the jockey telling him that he was going in the wrong direction. The only time the interpreter reacted to an inappropriate intervention by a monitor was when Miyamoto made the same mistake twice (see p.102 and p.119). In this case, the horse may have made a quick judgment to check the jockey before being led in a totally wrong direction.

Although the number of such incidents was very small, the interpreters, as we have seen, did interact directly with Tojo and the other participants to respond to their questions or to help them understand interpreting or procedural issues. Those exchanges were brief and concise and evidently fell within the scope of what would be tolerated by their supervisors.

The interpreters' efforts to render into English everything Tojo said are also apparent. The few instances in which the interpreters stopped the examiner from asking a new question indicate their eagerness to let Tojo complete his remarks. These observations suggest that whatever opinion an individual interpreter may have had of Tojo, they all made an effort to put him on an equal footing with those court participants who understood English. Asked if he ever tried to interpret to the advantage of the defense, even to the slightest extent, Shimada (2000, 28) responded, "I delivered to the advantage of the defense, but wouldn't everyone always do something like that, for his own country?" (the author's translation). Iwamoto, as we have also seen, is said to have applied for the interpreting job in order to be able to render a "last service" to the Emperor. While it is possible that the interpreters had a sense of professional ethics and thought that they ought to contribute to a fair trial, and it is also possible that some of them felt sympathy toward Tojo in particular or the defendants in general. In any event, however, they took care to act within the scope of what was tolerated by the court. The only time an interpreter may have gone too far was when one of them interrupted Keenan's question to explain that Tojo had not finished his response. Keenan then challenged the intervention, which may have deterred the interpreters from interrupting the speakers again (see p.117).

The monitors, meanwhile, were positioned in the middle of the hierarchy of the interpreting system. They monitored and supervised the Japanese interpreters, but they themselves were under the supervision of the chief of the Language Section. Considering that the language arbiter, and not the monitors, had the authority to make final rulings on language issues, the monitors were presumably positioned below the arbiter in the hierarchy as well. However, when it came to ability to understand and command both Japanese and English, the relative positions of the interpreters, the monitors, the language arbiter and the Language Section chief seem to have been reversed. Kraft's Japanese was at an elementary level, and Marvin R. Anderson, the Language Section chief at the time of Tojo's testimony, had studied Japanese for just six months in Saipan (Oka, 2008 email communication with the author, reports that he never heard Anderson speak Japanese during the trial). As for Anderson's deputy, Don C. Jones, the circumstances under which he was hired provide a glimpse of the level of Japanese proficiency among the supervisors in the Language Section. Jones had studied Japanese in Saipan as a Marine during the war, and then

> in the summer of 1947 he went to Washington, DC, seeking a language position. While [he was] in the Pentagon he saw a poster advertising, "Japanese Interpreters Wanted." He completed the required application and submitted to a physical examination, but, he said, "Nobody, not one person, asked me to speak a word of Japanese in the two days they processed me." Two weeks later he was on a ship to Japan. All the way there he worried about being found out. It wouldn't take long, he thought, before someone discovered the best he could do in Japanese was ask where the

restroom was. Aboard ship an acquaintance asked him to deliver a letter to a friend at SCAP in Tokyo. The friend turned out to be a colonel who was involved in the Class A war crimes trials. The colonel said to Jones, "We just lost the head of our language division. Can you handle the job?" Jones said, "Of course." And so he took a job with rank and pay equal to that of a colonel. During the trials, he delivered the oath in Japanese to witnesses and defendants. He ran the procedures of the trials as they related to interpreters. He was the administrator of the section and he had the best Japanese linguists the American and Japanese governments could supply. And nobody ever found out [that] he was "a phony." (Slesnick and Slesnick 2006, 313–15)

In practice, then, the monitors had a kind of power over their supervisors, to the extent that they had command of a language their supervisors barely understood. Thus, there were two layers of hierarchy, one explicit and the other implicit, in play between the interpreters, the monitors, the language arbiter and the Language Section chief: the institutional hierarchy and the hierarchy of bilingual capabilities.

Given these circumstances, it is interesting to consider why most of the monitors' interjections came in response to interpretations from English into Japanese. On the one hand, the Japanese interpreters may have had difficulty with legal terms and the language style specific to court proceedings in English, but they presumably had complete comprehension of utterances in Japanese (this view is shared by Watanabe 1998, 82). On the other hand, the *Nisei* monitors, apart from David Akira Itami, may have struggled to understand Japanese terms and the language styles specific to the Japanese military and the imperial court, but they presumably had full comprehension of utterances in English. This in itself may explain why most of their interjections related to English-to-Japanese interpretations: without understanding the source language, they could not hope to correct interpreting errors.

Another possible reason is that the monitors exercised self-restraint when it came to interpreting into English. When an interjection was uttered in English in response to a Japanese-to-English interpretation, the Tribunal could understand and compare the original interpretation by the interpreter with the monitor's version. The Tribunal was concerned about the time the proceedings were taking, as is mentioned in the transcripts and in a number of archival records, and probably did not have the patience to listen to two versions of an interpretation unless the difference was a material one. Being sensitive to their employers' needs, the monitors may have tended, consciously or unconsciously, to be more disciplined and selective about interjecting in English. This may also explain why their interjections in relation to Japanese-to-English interpretations often took the form of brief whispers. At the same time, it is possible that the monitors did not feel so inhibited about correcting errors or rephrasing in Japanese because of their awareness that their supervisors did not understand the language. Most court participants, including the language arbiter and the Language Section chief at the time of Tojo's testimony, simply did not have the capacity to judge if the monitors' interventions in Japanese were appropriate.

For example, a report prepared by a U.S. intelligence officer, Lieutenant Colonel William T. Hornaday Jr. (n. d.), describes the issues that the International Prosecution Section faced during the trial, and refers to interpreting as "the biggest single problem" both for the Section in particular and for the Tribunal in general. Hornaday adds that "Jap [sic] nationals [are] unsatisfactory unless monitored (Handicap, lack of knowledge of English)" and "US Niseis [sic] [are] unsatisfactory. Handicap—lack of knowledge of Japanese." If Hornaday was reporting the consensus within the Tribunal, as opposed to his own views, this may be evidence that the Tribunal did not have confidence in the Japanese interpreters and expected the Nisei monitors to compensate for the interpreters' deficiencies. On the other hand, Hornaday's assessments could have been based on his own or others' perception of what was going on in the interpreting booth, which may have given the impression that the monitors were busy correcting the interpreters' errors. Masakazu Shimada confirms (2000, 21) that the Tribunal was not aware of issues with the monitors because almost all the participants had little or no ability in Japanese and assumed that the monitors were effectively supervising the interpreters.

There are several possible reasons why the monitors rephrased interpretations even when they contained no errors or omissions. A given interpretation might have been delivered in such a way that it did not "sound right" to a monitor: as Gile (1999) suggests, assessments of the quality of interpreting varies depending on whether the data is presented in an audible form or in a transcription. Even if an interpretation "looks" fine and error-free in transcript, it may have "sounded" problematic to a monitor. In addition, these seemingly unnecessary interjections may be attributable to the monitors' inability to quickly and accurately evaluate the interpreters' performance. During Tojo's testimony, the average number per session of rephrasing interjections, mostly for English-to-Japanese interpretations, was six for Itami, eight and a half for Onodera and fifteen for Miyamoto. Itami had an appreciation of the variety of lexical and semantic usages in Japanese based on seventeen years of education in Japan and was probably better equipped than the other monitors to accept the wide range of word choices and language styles adopted in Japanese by the interpreters. The fact that Miyamoto, who had the weakest command of Japanese, rephrased interpretations far more frequently than the other monitors did and that Itami did so least frequently of all the monitors may support the argument that these seemingly unwarranted interjections occurred partly because of limitations in the monitors' knowledge of Japanese usages and vocabulary.

This aspect of the monitors' competence also leads to another possible reason for the seemingly unnecessary interjections: the monitors' eagerness to demonstrate their active involvement in the interpreting process. This seems especially applicable in the case of Miyamoto. The fact that he was eager to jump in to present his own versions of interpretations could be explained by his desire to prove that he was a functioning monitor despite his relative youth and his weak command of Japanese. The Language Section and the Tribunal were not capable of assessing his interjections and may have thought that he was busy correcting poor choices by the interpreters.

In contemporary courtrooms in the United States and many other countries, when interpreters make statements in their capacity as interpreters, the standard practice is for them to refer to themselves in the third person: "The interpreter would like to clarify with the witness," "By the interpreter: Could the court reporter repeat the question, please?" and so on (Mikkelson 2000, 50). During the Tokyo Trial, the clear division of labour, under which the interpreter interpreted and the monitor communicated any difficulty the interpreter might be experiencing, probably helped the court minimize confusion arising from interpreting issues. By the time Tojo gave his testimony, with Kraft as language arbiter, the monitors may have felt responsible for addressing language issues since they were the only people in the supervisory positions of the Language Section with any extensive Japanese proficiency. Because their supervisors did not understand the content of the monitors' interventions in Japanese, the monitors may have felt less inhibited about giving explanations to Tojo. In other words, by this late stage in the proceedings, if not earlier, the monitors were engaging in activities that were supposed to be performed by their supervisors, in ways that those supervisors would not be able to check.

Despite his position at the head of the hierarchy of the interpreting process, Kraft seems not to have made any significant impact on the proceedings. According to Lardner Moore (interviewed by his son in 1980), Kraft "had his own ideas about what's to be done" during the Language Arbitration Board's deliberations on language disputes, but in the courtroom his limited competence in Japanese probably prevented Kraft from being aware of the nature of the interjections in Japanese by the monitors and the interpreters, and he could not intervene in any of their activities. According to Yukio

Kawamoto (interviewed by the author in Springfield, Virginia, on March 20, 2005), Kraft was a "figurehead," limited to reporting the rulings of the Language Arbitration Board to the court. This is in contrast to Lardner Moore's active engagement with the court (as discussed in Chapter 4). Even as "a figurehead," however, the presence of Kraft, a Caucasian military officer, in the prosecution team's seating area, and his announcements of the rulings of the board in court may well have contributed to the appearance that the U.S. military was in charge of the proceedings of the Tokyo Trial. Based on the interviews and documents reviewed so far, it appears that during Tojo's testimony the higher a person was in the hierarchy of the linguists, the less competent that person was in his second language (Japanese or English). The Tribunal, however, continued to turn to the language arbiter to rule on disputed translations and interpretations.

As suggested above, the monitors' and interpreters' awareness that none of their supervisors fully understood the nature of their interjections in Japanese probably allowed the monitors and the interpreters to go beyond their basic duties of correcting errors and interpreting. Here, one may link their behaviour to what is known of their personal opinions about the trial and their attitudes to the defendants, although it should always be borne in mind that much of our evidence for their opinions or attitudes comes from interviews conducted many years after the Trial with men who may have revised their views in the meantime or whose memories were no longer entirely reliable.

Asked about his view of the trial, Takashi Oka (1998, 116–17), for example, responded that although he questioned the validity of automatically applying the framework of the Nuremberg Trials to a Japanese context that was totally different from that of Europe, he also conceded that the trial allowed the wartime activities of the Japanese military to be exposed more swiftly than would otherwise have been possible. Oka also stated, "Our policy-makers were just ordinary people," (the author's translation) as he observed some of the defendants showing unclear attitudes to taking responsibility for their wartime actions and trying to protect and justify themselves. Being the youngest interpreter and still in college, Oka was probably not in a position to even think about "helping" Tojo. In response to the question why some of the interpreters and monitors appeared to do so, he answered, "Well, I don't know." (2005, interview by the author)

Another former interpreter, Masakazu Shimada (2000, 28), recalls that he did try to interpret to the advantage of the defense, but he also describes a general atmosphere in which the interpreters and monitors tried not to discuss the trial and were very careful to keep their feelings to themselves out of fear that they would be reprimanded if they criticized the proceedings (Shimada 2000, 28, 30–32). Shimada also sensed that Itami, Onodera and Shimanouchi probably felt that "America [was] also at fault; it [was] terrible," (the author's translation) citing their experiences with the internment camps (Shimada 2000, 31). According to Kozo Kinashi (1985, 112; 2000, 41), Itami was critical of the Tokyo Trial; he "tried to protect the Emperor, and assisted Tojo as much as he could in his capacity as monitor, because he could see Tojo's quality as a sincere soldier" (the author's translation). Kinashi also claims that Itami "felt heavy" about having to see Shigenori Togo, his former benefactor, as a defendant in the trial (Kinashi 2000, 42).

However, these interviews and anecdotes do not provide any concrete examples of a link between the linguists' personal views of the trial and Tojo, and the ways in which they appeared to help him when he was giving his testimony. An attempt to search for such evidence in the transcripts has also proved inconclusive.

CHAPTER 6

SOCIOPOLITICAL PERSPECTIVES

Interpreting has been used to facilitate communication across languages and cultures throughout the history of humanity. Indeed, the history of interpreting is much longer than that of translation, since it must have taken place before the invention of writing systems.

Nevertheless, it did not become either widespread or institutionalized in international settings until the middle of the 20th century, when the profession of conference interpreting started to be developed and the need for training of interpreters grew in response to the unprecedented increase in international communication and interaction. Interpreting has further proliferated in recent decades as governments have started addressing the growing need for language assistance for immigrants, refugees and migrant workers in hospitals, courts and other settings.

Academic inquiries into interpreting have developed in the wake of these developments of the practice. Initially, and understandably, researchers focused mainly on conference interpreting, especially on issues of cognitive processing, drawing on such disciplines as psycholinguistics, cognitive psychology and neurolinguistics. However, over the past twenty years or so, the scope of interpreting studies has expanded rapidly to encompass more diverse interpreting settings and a wider range of theoretical approaches. In addition to studies that deal with professional issues, there are a number of studies, often influenced by sociolinguistics, discourse analysis and pragmatics, that focus on the interactional aspects of interpreting and the role of interpreters as communication mediators. There is also a growing interest in the sociocultural aspects of interpreting. For example, Michael Cronin (2002, 46) has called for a "cultural turn" in interpreting studies so that researchers pay more attention to "questions of power, and issues such as class, gender, race in interpreting situations." Franz Pöchhacker (2006) describes this evolution as a matter of interpreting studies "going social" and embracing more diverse forms of interpreting and broader contextualization.

This chapter attempts to apply this social approach to the findings from previous chapters in order to achieve a fuller and deeper understanding of the interpreting phenomena at the Tokyo Trial. Three sets of notions are deployed here: "trust, power and control" within the three-tier interpreting arrangements, as evidenced in the behaviour of some of the linguists; "autonomous" and "heteronomous" interpreters (Cronin 2002, 2006) to discuss the complex standing of the *Nisei* linguists; and the "negotiated norms" in the interpreting procedures developed during the initial stages of the proceedings.

Trust, Power and Control

When different parties represent different interests in an event mediated by interpreting, the party with the authority to select the interpreters will most likely choose interpreters who share the same interests and/or affiliations as that party or interpreters who are understood to be "neutral", and avoid using interpreters who seem to have a conflict of interest due to suspicions that they may act "in bad faith" or to advance their own agenda. Such suspicions arise from the "power" the interpreters are perceived to possess.

In discussing the role of interpreters, sociologist R. Bruce Anderson (1976, 218–21) presents a prototypical model of a bilingual interpreter working between two monolingual parties, then argues that "the interpreter's position as the person in the middle has the advantage of power inherent in all positions that control scarce resources," since the interpreter can monopolize the means of communication. However, Anderson's sociological model of interpreting perhaps oversimplifies the issues. In some cases, for example, an interpreter may be employed even when one or both of the parties can understand both languages in use, for various reasons, political, tactical or otherwise. A party may want to exercise its right to speak its own language instead of resorting to a lingua franca from the political standpoint of language equality. It may want to take advantage of consecutive interpreting so that it can gain extra time to think about its responses. It may seek to use the interpreter as a "cushion" when delivering a message that is unpleasant to the other party, or as a "scapegoat" to be blamed in the event of miscommunication.

This "irregular" model, in which an interpreter is used even when communication could have been achieved without him or her, can be seen, as Gideon Toury (2007, 31–34) points out, in the account in Genesis 41–43 of Joseph's meeting with his brothers, which is conducted via an interpreter, with Joseph speaking Egyptian and pretending he does not understand Hebrew. Mona Baker (1997) discusses the psychological and cultural constraints on those who interpret for political leaders with reference to Saddam Hussein using his own interpreter, as well as another interpreter to check on the first interpreter, when being interviewed for a British broadcaster, even though Hussein understood English. In such settings, where bilingual users of interpreting can check on the interpreter's work, the interpreter does not possess as much power to manipulate the communication as Anderson's model might suggest.

However, there are probably not many people who have the time or money to use interpreters in this particular way, and, just as in Anderson's model, it is usually the case that an interpreter is hired because the parties do not understand each other's language. In this context, it may be important for the monolingual user to be assured of the trustworthiness of the interpreter since they have no capacity to check on the fidelity of the interpretation.

Users' fears that interpreters may exercise their power to advance their own interests and manipulate the discourse are not completely unwarranted. Michael Cronin (2002, 55) gives the example of an interpreter in Ireland in the 18th century who deliberately misinterpreted the testimony given in Irish by a poet in a court where the official language was English. In 2004, a sign-language interpreter in Ukraine delivered her own political message on television while pretending to be interpreting election results (see Zarakhovich 2005). In both these cases, the party who hired the interpreter was presumably not aware of the interpreter's bad faith.

Mistrust arising out of an absence of shared interests or affiliations has been discussed throughout the history of interpreting. In the 13th century, William of Rubruck suspected that his Armenian interpreter was distorting his message (Bowen 1995, 254–55). In the early modern era envoys from Europe complained about the incompetence and disloyalty of Levantine dragomans in the Ottoman empire (Lewis 2004, 25–26). In Britain in 1820, the defense counsel at the trial of Queen Caroline expressed concern about the impartiality of the Italian interpreter provided by the prosecution (Morris 1999, 19). In Japan in 1853, the Shogunate did not permit John Manjiro, who had been teaching English to Japanese officials, to act as an interpreter in negotiations with Commodore Matthew Perry of the United States, since the Shogun's advisers suspected that Manjiro, who had spent nine years in the United States as a castaway, might side with the foreigners (Kato 2004,

77). More recently, in 2006, the inventor of IraqComm, a portable two-way interpreting device, suggested that human interpreters are not entirely to be trusted because they "may have their own agenda" (quoted in Abate 2006).

Given such suspicions, Rosalind Edwards and her co-authors (2005) find that trust is the key reason why some immigrants prefer to have relatives or friends, rather than professional interpreters, assist them in their interactions with social services. For certain assignments in government agencies, the top priority when hiring interpreters may be whether or not they are citizens or have been cleared in a security check, and not necessarily whether they are high-quality interpreters. As André Lefevere (1992, 2) suggests, "it is important to remember that trust is invested in the producer of the translation, not necessarily in the product itself," and in some political settings "trust may be more important than quality."

However, the number of "insider" interpreters is limited, and they may not be available all the time. Nor is there any guarantee that these insider interpreters will always work in good faith. Further, in order to make the communication effective and fulfil the purpose of the communication, the best available interpreters may be needed in some cases, even if they are "outsiders." Therefore, in order to ensure that competent interpreters act in good faith, the party with the authority to do so may establish a system to regulate and control the interpreters. In fact, there are some indications that systematic control of interpreters has existed since ancient times. For example, Ingrid Kurz (1985) discusses the princes of Elephantine in ancient Egypt as "overseers of dragomans," drawing on the earliest reference to interpreting, found in the princes' tombs. From 1529 to 1630, Spain issued a series of laws that specified the rates, working hours, ethics and penalties of interpreters who worked in the American colonies (Pym 1998b, 555). The *Oranda tsuji*, the Dutch interpreters in Japan during the Edo period (1600–1868), worked under stringent regulations and formed a hereditary profession in which only males from twenty-some designated families could take part (Torikai 2004, 274).

Such control over interpreters has been established not only to ensure the quality of their interpreting but also to address the concerns of monolingual users about the potential abuse of the power that bilingual interpreters possess, and to function as a deterrent against interpreters working in bad faith. Theo Hermans (2001, 4–7) discusses the work of interpreters during the European discovery of the Americas, as well as that of the *Oranda tsuji*, highlighting the "tight controls on translators and interpreters to guarantee their trustworthiness, to ensure that they speak exclusively with their masters' voice." Referring to the "overseers of the dragomans" in Ancient Egypt, Anthony Pym (1998a, 186) also draws attention to the institutionalization of translation: "hierarchical control is established; boundaries are maintained." According to Michael Cronin (2002, 58), "the role of interpreters throughout history has been crucially determined by the prevailing hierarchical constitution of power and their position in it." The codes of ethics and professional conduct to which interpreters are now expected to subscribe, based on such principles as neutrality, impartiality and fidelity, can be seen as means to gain and maintain the trust of clients and end-users by ensuring that interpreters do not exercise their power to manipulate discourse. Kathy Laster and Veronica Taylor (1994, 111) point to this power as the reason why lawyers try to regulate and constrain the role of interpreters as "neutral machines or conduits."

These sociopolitical aspects of interpreting—the perceived power of interpreters to manipulate communication, the suspicions of monolingual users that interpreters may exercise that power, the controls imposed on interpreters to deter them from doing so— were also in play during the Tokyo Trial. Given the interpreting arrangements that were made for the earlier war crimes trials in Manila and Yokohama (discussed in Chapter 4), it may be presumed that the Tokyo Tribunal also wanted to use U.S. military personnel as interpreters but found them incompetent and had to resort to using bilingual Japanese nationals. However, the Tribunal did not trust these Japanese interpreters to be impartial and was wary of appearing to depend on nationals of the very country whose former leaders were among the defendants: hence the three-part hierarchy of Japanese interpreters, *Nisei* monitors and U.S. Caucasian language arbiters discussed in detail in earlier chapters, which clearly represents the desire of the party with authority over the proceedings to regulate and control interpreters who did not necessarily share its interests or affiliations. The hierarchy among the linguists at the Tokyo Trial functioned as a display of authority and a check against any possibility of bad faith affecting communication.

There was also a system to monitor interpreting at the Nuremberg Trial. According to Francesca Gaiba (1998, 77–82), a monitor sat at the end of the interpreters' table during the proceedings to check the accuracy of the interpreting, the degree to which interpreters might be becoming fatigued, the volume of speakers' utterances and the operation of the interpreting equipment. The monitor also took charge of the documents provided to the interpreters, and acted as liaison between them and the court. In contrast to the Tokyo Trial, which relied on consecutive interpreting, the Nuremberg Trial used simultaneous interpreting between four languages, so it was rarely the case that the proceedings were stopped so that errors could be discussed and corrected. Instead, the interpreters themselves corrected their own errors by checking the daily transcripts against the verbatim recordings (Gaiba 1998, 71, 97–98. According to Peter Less (2005), who was one of the interpreters at Nuremberg, the interpreters also "cleaned up" some vulgar and crude language. At the Nuremberg Trial, people who might have shared the Nazi affiliations of the defendants were not permitted to engage in interpreting, so, perhaps, the trustworthiness of the interpreters was not as much of an issue as it was in Tokyo. It seems more reasonable to characterize this monitoring system as a means to ensure the smooth operation of the interpreting arrangements in a formal international setting during the nascent stage of simultaneous interpreting, rather than as a means to police the interpreters' behaviour.

Exhibit 6.1 Interpreters at Nuremberg, supervised by a monitor (right)

The behaviour of some of the monitors and interpreters at the Tokyo Trial (as discussed in Chapter 5) demonstrated that they also exerted a degree of power in the awareness that their users and supervisors were monolingual. For instance, when monitors or interpreters provided explanations and advisory comments to Tojo in Japanese, neither the language arbiter nor the Language Section chief was sufficiently competent in the language to check what they were saying. Thus, even when a monitor or, occasionally, an interpreter behaved outside the ethical standards generally subscribed to by court interpreters nowadays—such as the prohibitions on adding information, editing interpretations or communicating directly with a speaker without the court's permission—the supervisors were in no position to point out that a line was being crossed, to warn against transgressions or to reprimand the monitor or interpreter, so long as Japanese was being used.

Given the highly political nature of the proceedings, the Tokyo Trial may be considered an exceptional case, and certainly it is necessary to exercise caution in generalizing what happened there. Nonetheless, the way in which the three-tier interpreting system was devised, and the interpreters and monitors behaved during the proceedings, may be taken as a paradigm of how issues of power, trust and control may play out in any event that is mediated through interpreters.

Autonomous and Heteronomous Interpreters

During the era of discoveries, from the 15th century to the 17th century, interpreters proved to be indispensable to the expeditions and colonial operations of Spain, Portugal and other European countries. Michael Cronin (2002, 55–58; 2006, 101–02, 114–15) discusses two ways in which the explorers and colonizers procured and trained their interpreters. First, "heteronomous interpreters" were recruited from among native peoples, by force or through inducements, and then taught the colonizer's language. La Malinche (also known as Doña Marina), who was the interpreter/assistant to Hernán Cortés during the Spanish conquest of Mexico, may be the best-known example. Other heteronomous interpreters became sources of concern to colonizers because of their knowledge of the languages and cultures of both lands. Cronin (2002, 57) refers to the case of Orundellico (also known as Jeremy or Jemmy Button), who was taken from Tierra del Fuego, perhaps by force, by the English crew of HMS *Beagle* in 1830 and was taught English in England, and then returned three years later to Tierra del Fuego, where he regained "nativeness" immediately, and became manipulative and dangerous for the English.

Concern about the reliability of heteronomous interpreters contributed to the shift toward using "autonomous interpreters," selected from the populations of the colonial metropoles and trained in the languages of the colonized. Cronin (2002, 57–58) gives the example of Samuel de Champlain, who, during his exploration in the early 17th century of what is now the province of Quebec, sent young Frenchmen to live among the indigenous peoples and learn their languages. Following this experiment, in 1669 the French court arranged to have French-born children trained in Turkish, Arabic and Persian (Farsi).

The shift from heteronomous to autonomous interpreting can also be observed in the contacts between the government of the Ottoman empire and the embassies of the various European powers in Istanbul (Lewis 2004, 24–28). Initially, the Ottoman officials used renegades—Hungarians, Poles, Germans or Italians who had abandoned Christianity—but after 1661 they employed "dragomans," Greek subjects of the Sultan who had been sent to Italy for schooling. The European embassies, meanwhile, relied on Levantines, mainly Catholics of Italian origin living in Turkey who were also subjects of the Sultan. Like the dragomans, these interpreters were outsiders in Ottoman society, being Christians rather than Muslims, and yet they were also outsiders from the perspective of their European employers. Accordingly, they were regarded with suspicion and were sometimes accused of selling their services to the highest bidder, exchanging secrets with their colleagues or counterparts on the other side, selling secrets they had obtained on the job, or being too afraid of the Ottoman authorities to perform their functions effectively.

Eventually, the European embassies shifted to using autonomous interpreters, recruited from among their own peoples. These young Englishmen, Frenchmen, Austrians and Russians started working with the Levantine interpreters but eventually replaced them as the heteronomous interpreting system faded away. On the Ottoman side, a similar shift to autonomous interpreting was heralded in 1821 with the execution of the chief interpreter, the Grand Dragoman, on the grounds that he had supported the Greeks in their war of independence. From then on, non-Muslims were no longer appointed as interpreters, and the Ottoman government established a translation office, staffed entirely by Turks, which was made responsible not only for translating and interpreting but also for drafting diplomatic documents and implementing foreign policy, and which eventually "became the main avenue to power in Turkish bureaucratic politics" (Lewis 2004, p. 28).

Autonomous interpreters given other functions in government and diplomacy were not limited to the Ottoman empire. The *Oranda tsuji* of Japan provide another example. After the Shogunate imposed its "seclusion policy" in the 1630s, and Dutch traders became the only Westerners permitted to have contact with Japan, it established a system in which only members of about twenty designated families could become official Dutch interpreters. These interpreters were government officials and could be punished if they acted against policy. In 1829, for example, after Philipp Franz von Siebold, a German physician employed by the Dutch, was found to have obtained maps of Japan and was expelled from the country, the *Oranda tsuji* who had worked with him were charged with treason and severely punished (Torikai 2004, 265–67). The *Oranda tsuji* were also engaged in administering the trade with the Netherlands, checking the crews and the cargos on Dutch ships calling at Nagasaki, and some of them gathered information on world affairs from the Dutch traders, becoming pioneers of the introduction of Western science and technologies into Japan.

These examples of the Ottoman interpreters and the *Oranda tsuji* suggest that one of the differences between autonomous and heteronomous interpreters can be found in whether or not they engage in administrative functions in addition to working as interpreters. The same question may be asked about the Japanese interpreters, the *Nisei* monitors and the Caucasian language arbiters at the Tokyo Trial. Obviously, the Japanese interpreters were "heteronomous," being, from the perspective of the Tribunal, "natives" who were procured locally. It is also clear that, in relation to the Tribunal, the Caucasian language arbiters were "autonomous." Lardner Moore had been born and raised in Japan and did not receive any training from the U.S. military, but Edward Kraft was a quintessential "autonomous interpreter," having been trained at the Military Intelligence Service Language School and in preparatory courses at University of Michigan.

However, the case of the *Nisei* linguists is more complex. They were "autonomous" in the sense that they were U.S. citizens recruited and trained by the U.S. military. Since the monitors were *Kibei*, they also had some "heteronomous" characteristics. Their education and experience in Japan had been prompted by their "native" parents, not by the U.S. military, and they had been recruited as military linguists "through inducements," in their case to get out of or avoid internment and prove their loyalty to the United States. Thus, from the perspective of the Tribunal the *Nisei* monitors were "autonomous" by affiliation, but they were also "heteronomous" and therefore open to the suspicion that they might become too sympathetic to the Japanese defendants. The monitors supervised the Japanese interpreters inside the booth, but feedback concerning the interpreting procedures was communicated via the Language Section chief and the language arbiter during the initial stages of the proceedings, and the monitors were not given any other administrative tasks. In short, the *Nisei* monitors, being both autonomous and heteronomous, were "in between."

Negotiated Norms

Gideon Toury (1995, 241–58) provides a model of norms for natural/native interpreters, that is, bilinguals who develop their interpreting skills on the job without any prior professional training. (Toury actually uses the term "translators," but the focus of his discussion appears to be on interpreters, and that is the term that will be used here.) The personnel who were involved in the interpreting process at the Tokyo Trial fit Toury's definition, and the aim of this section is to illustrate the interactive aspect of the negotiation of the norms for their work and their cognitive constraints as a factor in that process.

Toury's (1978/2000) concept of "norms" has been one of the most influential concepts in translation studies. He developed it, mainly in the context of literary translation, to refer to regularities in translational behaviour. His view of translation as a norm-governed activity has inspired many translation researchers to focus on the target text and culture instead of on the correspondence between the source text and the target text; to describe and explain translational activities based on empirical research instead of prescribing them; and to pay attention to the sociological and cultural aspects of translational phenomena beyond the linguistic features of texts. The notion of translational norms has also been applied in the field of interpreting research to address methodological questions in the identifying of interpreting norms (Shlesinger 1989), to identify interpreting norms based on professional observation (Harris 1990) and to undertake empirical studies (Jansen 1995; Schjoldager 1995/2002; Diriker 2004). These studies have also dealt with the difficulty of separating norm-governed features of interpreting from those attributable to interpreters' cognitive constraints (Shlesinger 1999, 2001), and the interactive aspects of norm-building and the status of interpreters, drawing on sociological concepts (Inghilleri 2003, 2005). Of particular interest is the argument put forward by Daniel Gile (1998, 100) that "interpreting strategies are at least partly norm-based," although "many of them primarily address cognitive constraints," and that norms can vary depending on settings and perspectives, such as interpreters' own views of their performance or users' expectations of interpreters' performance.

Toury (1995, 241–59) refers to an interpreting phenomenon by drawing on the notion of translation norms. In describing how a bilingual speaker grows into the role of an interpreter without formal training, Toury points to the internalization of feedback from the interpreter's environment, in a process that is also referred to as "socialization." Toury acknowledges the interactional aspect of communicative activity, which involves feedback from various players such as the receiver of the translated utterance, the originator of the utterance and the commissioner of the communicative event. According to Toury, such feedback embodies norms that determine not only the appropriateness or inappropriateness of various aspects of the interpreting activity but also the sanctioning of certain inappropriate behaviours because they do not conform to norms. Toury argues that those who internalize feedback and conform to the acquired norms will be recognized as having become interpreters.

The interpreters at the Tokyo Trial were all "natural/native interpreters" in Toury's sense. They were bilingual because of their family, educational and/or professional backgrounds, but none of them had ever received formal training to become interpreters. Although they received some orientation on court procedures after being recruited, there was virtually no training for interpreting as such before they started work in the courtroom, and they had to learn on the job over the course of the trial. Many of them dropped out in the early stages, but several became functioning interpreters. In addition to gaining interpreting skills, they experienced the "socialization" that Toury refers to.

The feedback that the interpreters received, and that contributed to this process of socialization, came in the form of comments, requests or orders from the President of the Tribunal, Sir William Webb, and other participants, including the prosecutors, defense counsel, defendants and other witnesses. However, the interpreters did not simply internalize this feedback and conform to the norms, as Toury's model might suggest. Instead, they responded to the feedback and explained their inability to accept certain norms. Their responses were conveyed mainly through the language arbiter and the chief of the Language Section, as in principle they were not supposed to speak on their own behalf, but the content of their responses is clear even so.

The Tribunal, in its capacity as commissioner and user of the interpreters, presumably expected the interpreters to conform to certain norms from the beginning of the proceedings, but these norms were adjusted over time in response to the interpreters' needs, which were largely based on their cognitive constraints, such as their inability to interpret excessively long passages, or their difficulties with interpreting prepared statements when they did not have prior access to translations. In order to move forward with the court proceedings, the Tribunal had to come to terms with these unfamiliar constraints and accommodate the interpreters' needs and requirements. What resulted was a *negotiation* of norms, between the interpreters and the user of their services, that is absent from Toury's model. The "expectancy norms" (Chesterman 1993, 9–11) that the Tribunal had tried to enforce at the beginning of the proceedings gave way to adjusted norms formulated in response to the feedback from the interpreters, and that indicates what is missing from Toury's model: the interpreters' participation in the interactional aspect of norm-building (Toury 1995, 248). In subsequent work Toury (1998, 15, 20) does acknowledge that norms can result from constant negotiations over what is to be agreed upon within a given group, and suggests an inquiry into whether interpreters have power to negotiate norms, but as Anthony Pym (1998c, 113) has pointed out, this is just a reflection of Toury's initial interest in who may participate in the negotiation of norms. There is much work that remains to be done to focus on the people involved in the negotiation process.

In interpreted events, especially in settings where dialogue is being interpreted, the involvement of the interpreter is more noticeable than that of translators because of the immediacy of the interactional discourse. As Cecilia Wadensjö argues throughout her influential book *Interpreting as Interaction* (1998), the interpreter is an engaged participant in the interactional discourse of the interpreted event. Moira Inghilleri (2003, 2005) also shows a keen awareness of this interactional aspect of interpreting in her discussion of the formation of interpreting norms in the setting of asylum hearings. In order to reflect interpreters' involvement in the negotiation of norms, Toury's model of natural/native interpreters should therefore be extended to include feedback from the interpreters to their commissioners and users.

It should also be noted that norms develop as part of the rationalizing of the cognitive constraints of interpreters (Shlesinger 1999, 73) such as those that affected the interpreting of long passages and prepared statements at the Tokyo Trial (as mentioned above). The way in which simultaneous interpreters work in teams and take turns can be considered as a norm developed in response to interpreters' cognitive constraints, since they cannot maintain quality performance for an extended period of time. Interpreters' cognitive constraints form another aspect of interpreting that is not covered by Toury's model.

Finally, as we have seen (in Chapter 4), the interpreting procedures at the Tokyo Trial were devised and established through the exchanges between the interpreters and the users of their service about their requirements and expectations. Through this process, both the interpreters and the users became functioning participants in an interpreter-mediated event. This suggests that "the making of a native/natural translator" (or interpreter) to which Toury (1995, 248) refers is also a matter of "making" the users of the interpreter.

Conclusion

This book has described the interpreting arrangements at the Tokyo Trial and presented a sociopolitical analysis of their distinctive features and of the behaviour of some of the linguists, in particular during the testimony of Hideki Tojo. Drawing on a wide variety of materials, including previously classified documents and interviews with some of the linguists, this book has provided new information on an important trial that has been somewhat neglected in previous studies of the history of interpreting. It has also highlighted the political context of the trial and the social and cultural backgrounds of the linguists as key factors in the selection of the linguists, the procedures of interpreting and the behaviour of some of the linguists.

Two points as to the historical significance of the Tokyo Trial are worth making in closing. One concerns the position of the Tokyo Trial in the history of conference interpreting in Japan, the other concerns the historical parallels and comparisons between the experiences of the *Nisei* linguists who worked at the Tokyo Trial and the circumstances being faced by some of the military linguists currently serving in Iraq and Afghanistan.

The Tokyo Trial and Interpreting in Japan

The Tokyo Trial was an international forum involving people from more than ten countries, and, in addition to English and Japanese, Chinese, Russian, German, French, Dutch and Mongolian were also spoken during the proceedings (as discussed in Chapter 2). The interpreting, therefore, had some characteristics of the "conference" mode rather than the "dialogue" mode, involving a relatively large number of multilingual participants and formal meeting procedures. Relay interpreting, which is often used in conference settings, was also used at the Tokyo Trial. It is possible that before the trial there had been meetings at which Japanese and two or more other languages were spoken, with relay interpreting, but this was the first time that dedicated interpreters, rather than delegates or other participants present for other purposes, engaged in the task of interpreting in a booth with simultaneous interpreting equipment over a long period of time. The interpreting at the Tokyo Trial should therefore be considered as a precursor to conference interpreting in Japan.

At the same time, it should be acknowledged that some essential aspects of conference interpreting were missing from the Tokyo Trial. For example, while the first Nuremberg Trial is often cited as a milestone in the history of conference interpreting, or as "the coming of age" (Baigorri Jalón 1999, 34) of simultaneous interpreting, the Tokyo Trial involved consecutive interpreting, and the interpreters who worked during its proceedings did not become involved in the professionalization of conference interpreting in Japan (see Torikai 2009). Thus, in Japan there was no linear development of the profession of interpreting equivalent to the development of simultaneous conference interpreting from Nuremberg to the United Nations and beyond.

Nevertheless, the Tokyo Trial should be regarded as an important event in the history of interpreting in Japan, since the Japanese public became familiar with the system of interpreting over the course of the proceedings, and even gained some impression of what simultaneous interpreting would be like from reports and photographs in the press of court participants wearing headsets to listen to translations of prepared statements. The Tokyo Trial also provided an unprecedented amount of data on interpreting between English and Japanese, and may in fact be the source of the largest corpus of interpreting between these two languages to date.

Contemporary Parallels

Anthony Pym (1998a, x) has argued that "we do translation history in order to express, address and try to solve problems affecting our own situation." In this light, the extraordinary experiences of the *Nisei* monitors discussed in previous chapters may shed some light on the issues faced by military interpreters today.

To begin with, some parallels and comparisons may be drawn between the backgrounds of the *Nisei* linguists who worked at the Tokyo Trial and the situations of some of the linguists currently serving with the U.S. military. In both cases, an event of historic magnitude (the Japanese attack on Pearl Harbor and the terrorist attacks on 9/11) prompted the U.S. government to recruit and train interpreters and translators (of Japanese in the early 1940s and of Arabic, Dari, Farsi, Urdu, Kurdish, Pashto, and other languages today) for its military and intelligence operations. In both cases, some of these linguists were recruited from among groups that the U.S. government previously viewed as dangerous enemies. In the contemporary case, U.S.-born soldiers have been trained in languages almost from scratch (as "autonomous interpreters"), mainly at the Defense Language Institute in Monterey, California, which originated in the Military Intelligence Service Language School, but the military has also been relying on private contractors to supply locally hired linguists ("heteronomous interpreters"). In 2007, the U.S. Army's Intelligence and Security Command awarded new five-year contracts, worth more than US\$ 5 billion in total, to three companies to supply thousands of interpreters and translators in Iraq and Afghanistan, and at the detention facility in Guantanamo (see Defense Industry Daily 2007).

The U.S. military is also recruiting first-generation immigrants or foreign-born speakers of what the Defense Language Transformation Roadmap of 2005 calls "emerging languages" and teaching them English so that they can be deployed as interpreters and translators in conflict zones (see Schafer 2007). These foreign-born military linguists are "natives" in the sense that they were born and have lived in countries where Arabic, Dari, Pashto, and other "emerging languages" are in use, but they are now residents of the United States, whether as citizens or as permanent resident aliens. They are recruited and trained by the U.S. military, and are members of the U.S. forces, and in this regard they may be considered "insiders." Nevertheless, their ambivalent standing seems similar to that of the *Nisei* and especially the *Kibei* linguists during the Pacific War. Just as the *Nisei* linguists had to overcome difficult and complex challenges while working as interpreters and translators, it is possible that some military linguists today face similar problems in Iraq and Afghanistan. In fact, there have been articles in the press that offer snippets of information on the difficulties they have experienced (see, for example, Glionna and Khalil 2005; Packer 2007). On the one hand, they do not seem to be fully trusted by the U.S. government because of their cultural backgrounds and previous affiliations but, on the other hand, they are being placed in dangerous situations in which they may be viewed as traitors and targeted for intimidation or even retaliation (for a more extensive discussion, see Takeda 2009).

The experience of the *Nisei* linguists is not, then, an isolated case. In times of conflict, interpreters whose allegiances may be questioned, because of their connections with the languages and cultures of both warring parties, may face complex and difficult challenges, both physical and psychological, involving issues of trust and cultural identity.

Broadening Perspectives

The focus throughout this book has been placed on interpreters and other linguists, with close attention being paid to their social and cultural backgrounds, and the historical and political contexts that brought them to the Tokyo Trial. The findings have reaffirmed the view that interpreting, as a social practice, should be described and explained with attention to its contextual factors, beyond mere microlinguistic analysis. Although the Tokyo Trial may be considered a unique case because of its highly political nature, some of the issues this book has sought to address—such as the trustworthiness, power, ethics and control of interpreters, and the interactional aspects of norm-building—can be extended to interpreting in other settings. It is the author's hope that these issues will be revisited in future research so that there may be a fuller and more enhanced understanding of interpreting phenomena.

References

Abate, Tom. (2006, May 29). "Military Getting High-Tech Help from SRI Lab." *San Francisco Chronicle.* Online at http://www.sfgate.com/cgi-bin/article.cgi?file=/c/a/2006/05/29/BUGF8J39HK1.DTL [consulted March 22, 2010].

Anderson, R. Bruce. (1976). "Perspectives on the Role of Interpreter," in *Translation: Applications and Research*, ed. Richard W. Brislin. New York: Gardner Press, pp. 208–28.

Asahi Shimbun Hotei-kisha-dan. (1948). *Tokyo Saiban I.* Tokyo: News-sha. ———. (1949). *Tokyo Saiban II.* Tokyo: News-sha.

Asahi Shimbun Tokyo saiban kisha-dan. (1995). *Tokyo Saiban.* Tokyo: Asahi Shimbun-sha.

Awaya Kentaro. (2006). *Tokyo Saiban e no Michi.* Tokyo: Kodansha.

Baigorri Jalón, Jesús. (1999). "Conference Interpreting: From Modern Times to Space Technology." *Interpreting* 4:1, pp. 29–40.

Baker, Mona. (1997). "Non-Cognitive Constraints and Interpreter Strategies," in *Translating Sensitive Texts*, ed. Karl Simms. Amsterdam and Atlanta, GA: Rodopi, pp. 111–29.

Barik, Henri C. (1975/2002). "Simultaneous Interpretation: Qualitative and Linguistic Data," in *Interpreting Studies Reader*, ed. Franz Pöchhacker and Miriam Shlesinger. London and New York: Routledge, pp. 79–91.

Berk-Seligson, Susan. (1990/2002). *The Bilingual Courtroom: Court Interpreters in the Judicial Process*. Chicago and London: University of Chicago Press.

Bigham, William. (2003, Fall). "Unparalleled Patriotism: Japanese-Americans in World War II." *World War II Chronicles* issue 22. Online at http://www.americanveteranscenter.org/magazine/wwiichronicles/issue-xxii-fall-2003/unparalelled-patriotism-japanese-americans-in-world-war-ii/ [consulted March 22, 2010].

Bishop, H. C. (1948). *Roster of Department of the Army Civilian Linguists for Far East Command as of 31 December, 1948*. Records of the Allied Operational and Occupation Headquarters, World War II (Records Group 331), U.S. National Archives.

Bix, Herbert P. (2000). *Hirohito and the Making of Modern Japan*. New York: Perennial.

Bowen, Margareta, et al. (1995). "Interpreters and the Making of History," in *Translators through History*, ed. Jean Delisle and Judith Woodsworth. Amsterdam and Philadelphia: John Benjamins, pp. 245–80.

Brackman, Arnold C. (1987). *The Other Nuremberg: The Untold Story of the Tokyo War Crimes Trials*. New York: William Morrow.

Bradsher, Greg. (n. d.) *Select Findings Aid to Records at the National Archives at College Park, Maryland, Relating to Japanese War Crimes, War Criminals and War Crimes Trials: Post-war Restitution and Reparations; and to the Capture and Exploitations of Japanese Records and After WWII*. College Park, MD: U.S. National Archives Textual Archives Services Division.

———. (2005). "The 'Z Plan' Story: Japan's 1944 Naval Battle Strategy Drifts into U.S. Hands, Part 2." *NARA-Prologue* 37:3. Online at http://www.archives.gov/publications/prologue/2005/fall/zplan2.html [consulted March 22, 2010].

———. (2006). "The Exploitation of Captured and Seized Japanese Records Relating to War Crimes, 1942–1945," in *Researching Japanese War Crimes Records*. Washington, DC: Nazi War Crimes and Japanese Imperial Government Records Interagency Working Group, pp. 151–68.

Chesterman, Andrew. (1993). "From 'Is' to 'Ought': Translation Laws, Norms and Strategies." *Target* 5:1, pp. 1–20.

Cronin, Michael. (2002). "The Empire Talks Back: Orality, Heteronomy, and the Cultural Turn in Interpretation Studies," in *Translation and Power*, ed. Maria Tymoczko and Edwin Gentzler. Amherst and Boston: University of Massachusetts Press, pp. 45–62.

———. (2006). *Translation and Identity*. London and New York: Routledge.

Defense Industry Daily. (2007, December 10). "L-3 Out, Dyncorp-McNeil In for $4.65B Iraq Translation Contract?" Online at http://www.defenseindustrydaily.com/l3-out-dyncorpmcneil-in-for-465b-iraq-translation-contract-02885/ [consulted March 22, 2010].

Densho Digital Archive. *Military Intelligence Service*. Online at http://archive.densho.org/main.aspx [consulted June 15, 2010].

Diriker, Ebru. (2004). *De/Re-Contextualizing Conference Interpreting*. Amsterdam and Philadelphia: John Benjamins.

Dower, John. (1999). *Embracing Defeat: Japan in the Wake of World War II*. New York: W. W. Norton.

Drea, Edward. (2006). Introduction, in *Researching Japanese War Crimes Records*. Washington, DC: Nazi War Crimes and Japanese Imperial Government Records Interagency Working Group, pp. 3–20.

Edwards, Rosalind, et al. (2005). "Users' Experiences of Interpreters: The Critical Role of Trust." *Interpreting* 7:1, pp. 77–95.

Fuji Nobuo. (1988). *Watashi no mita Tokyo saiban*. Tokyo: Kodansha.

Gaiba, Francesca. (1998). *The Origins of Simultaneous Interpretation: The Nuremburg Trial*. Ottawa: University of Ottawa Press.

Gesse, Tanya. (2005, January–February, "Lunch with a Legend." *Communicate*. Online at http://www.aiic.net/ViewPage.cfm/page1665.htm [consulted March 22, 2010].

Gile, Daniel. (1998). "Norms in Research on Conference Interpreting: A Response to Theo Hermans and Gideon Toury." *Current Issues in Language and Society* 5:1 & 2, pp. 99–106.

———. (1999). "Variability in the Perception of Fidelity in Simultaneous Interpretation." *Hermes* 22, pp. 51–79.

Glionna, John M., and Ashraf Khalil. (2005, June 5). "'Combat Linguists' Battle on Two Fronts." *Los Angeles Times*. Online at http://articles.latimes.com/2005/jun/05/world/fg-interpret5 [consulted March 22, 2010].

Hale, Sandra Beatriz. (2004). *The Discourse of Court Interpreting*. Amsterdam and Philadelphia: John Benjamins.

Harries, Meirion, and Susie Harries. (1989). *Sheathing the Sword: The Demilitarization of Japan*. New York/London: Macmillan/Heinemann.

Harris, Brian. (1990). "Norms in Interpretation." *Target* 2:1, pp. 115–19.

Hermans, Theo. (2001). "Shall I Apologize Translation?" *Journal of Translation Studies* 5, pp. 1–18. Online at http://eprints.ucl.ac.uk/516/ [consulted March 22, 2010].

Hewitt, William E. (1995). *Court Interpretation: Model Guides for Policy and Practice in the State Courts*. Williamsburg, VA: National Center for State Courts.

Hornaday, Lt. Col. William T., Jr. (n. d.). "Outline of Talk on IPS by Lt. Col. Hornaday." Records of the Allied Operations and Occupation in Headquarters, WWII, U.S. National Archives.

Horowitz, Solis. (1950). "The Tokyo Trial." International Conciliation 465, p. 538.

Hosokawa, Bill. (1969/2002). *Nisei: The Quiet Americans*. Boulder, CO: University of Colorado Press.

Ichioka Yuji. (2006). *Before Internment: Essays in Prewar Japanese American History*. Stanford, CA: Stanford University Press.

IMDb [Internet Movie Database]. (n. d.) "Sho Onodera." Online at http://www.imdb.com/name/nm0648792/. [consulted March 22, 2010].

IMTFE [International Military Tribunal for the Far East]. (1946–1948). Transcripts of the Proceedings of the International Military Tribunal for the Far East. U.S. National Archives; also Public Record Office, Kew, London, FO 648/1-160.

———. (1948). *The Judgment of the International Military Tribunal for the Far East*. Online at http://ibiblio.org/hyperwar/PTO/IMTFE/index.html [consulted March 22, 2010].

Inghilleri, Moira. (2003). "Habitus, Field and Discourse: Interpreting as a Socially Situated Activity." *Target* 15:2, pp. 243–68.

Inghilleri, Moira. (2005). "The Sociology of Bourdieu and the Construction of the 'Object' in Translation and Interpreting Studies." *Translator* 11:2, pp. 125–45.

Itami, David Akira. (1949/1987). *Hennen-shiki kubun-shiki Ichidaiki* ["Personal Chronology," handwritten in 1949], in *Ryumon*, ed. Kajiki High School, p.42.

Jansen, Peter. (1995). "The Role of the Interpreter in Dutch Courtroom Interaction: The Impact of the Situation on Translational Norms," in *Topics in Interpreting Research*, ed. Jorma Tommola. Turku: University of Turku Centre for Translation and Interpreting, pp. 11–36.

Kato Yuzo. (2004). *Bakumatsu Gaiko to Kaikoku*. Tokyo: Chikuma Shinsho.

Keene, Donald. (2008). *Chronicles of My Life: An American in the Heart of Japan*. New York: Columbia University Press [based on articles first published in the *Daily Yomiuri* in 2006 and no longer available online].

Kinashi Kozo. (1985). *Dave Itami Akira no Shogai: Kyokuto Kokusai Gunji Saiban Hishi*. Tokyo: Paru Shuppan.

———. (2000). "Hakuun raikyo." *Daito Forum* 13, pp. 37–49.

Kojima Noboru. (1971). *Tokyo Saiban*. Tokyo: Chuko Shinsho.

Komatsu Tatsuya. (2003). *Tsuyaku no eigo nihongo*. Tokyo: Bungei Shunju.

Kono Rikako. (2003). "The Identity of a *Kibei-Nisei*: The Life of Akira Itami." *Ferris Wheel* 6, pp. 82–102.

Konosu Yukiko. (2005). *Meiji Taisho honyaku wonderland*. Tokyo: Shinchosha.

Kurz, Ingrid. (1985). "The Rock Tombs of the Princes of Elephantine: Earliest References to Interpretation in Pharaonic Egypt." *Babel* 31:4, pp. 213–18.

Kyokuto kokusai gunji saiban sokkiroku. (1968). Tokyo: Yushodo Shoten.

Laster, Kathy, and Veronica Taylor. (1994). *Interpreters and the Legal System*. Leichhardt, NSW: Federation Press.

Lefevere, André. (1992). Introduction, in *Translation/History/Culture*, ed. Lefevere. London and New York: Routledge.

Less, Peter. (2005, November 10). "Speaking with a History Maker: Interpreters at the Nuremberg Trials." Presentation at the American Translators Association Conference, Seattle, WA.

Lewis, Bernard. (2004). *From Babel to Dragomans: Interpreting the Middle East*. Oxford: Oxford University Press.

Maga, Timothy P. (2001). *Judgment at Tokyo: The Japanese War Crimes Trials*. Lexington: University Press of Kentucky.

Masaki Hideki. *(1992). Showa tenno no omoide: Sokkin tsuyaku 25-nen.* Tokyo: Yomiuri Shimbun-sha.

Massachusetts Court System. (1988). *Code of Professional Conduct for Court Interpreters of the Trial Court*. Online at http://www.mass.gov/courts/admin/planning/codeofconduct.html [consulted March 22, 2010].

McNaughton, James C. (1994). "*Nisei* Linguists and New Perspectives on the Pacific War: Intelligence, Race, and Continuity." Online at http://www.history.army.mil/html/topics/apam/Nisei.htm [consulted March 22, 2010].

———. (2006). Nisei *Linguists: Japanese Americans in the Military Intelligence Service During World War II*. Washington, DC: Department of the Army.

Mikkelson, Holly. (2000). *Introduction to Court Interpreting*. Northampton, MA, and Manchester: St. Jerome Publishing.

Military Intelligence Service Resource Center. "Video Gallery." Online at http://www.njahs.org/misnorcal/resources/resources_videos.htm [consulted March 22, 2010].

Minear, Richard H. (1971). *Victor's Justice: The Tokyo War Crimes Trial*. Princeton, NJ: Princeton University Press.

Morris, Ruth. (1999). "The Gum Syndrome: Predicaments in Court Interpreting." *Forensic Linguistics* 1:1, pp. 6–29.

Moser-Mercer, Barbara. (2005). "The Teaching of Simultaneous Interpreting: The First 60 Years (1929–1989)." *Forum* 3:1, pp. 205–25.

NHK [Nippon Hoso Kyokai]. (2006, August 10 and 14). *Nihon to tatakatta nikkei-jin*. Television documentary.

Niiya, Brian, ed. (2001). *Encyclopedia of Japanese American History: An A to Z Reference from 1868 to the Present*. New York: Facts on File.

Oka Takashi. (1998, October). "Tokyo saiban hotei tsuyaku no shogen." *This is Yomiuri*, pp. 116–17.

Otake Tomoko. (2005, August 14). "Between Two Worlds: Tried to the Limit and Beyond." *Japan Times*.

Packer, George. (2007, March 26). "Betrayed: The Iraqis who Trusted America the Most." *New Yorker*, pp. 52–73.

Pal, Radhabinod. (1953). *International Military Tribunal for the Far East: Dissentient Judgment*. Calcutta: Sanyal.

Pöchhacker, Franz. (2004). *Introducing Interpreting Studies*. London and New York: Routledge.

———. (2006). "Going 'Social'?" in *Sociocultural Aspects of Translation*, ed. Anthony Pym et al. Amsterdam and Philadelphia: John Benjamins, pp. 223–32.

Pritchard, R. John, ed. (1998 onward). *The Tokyo Major War Crimes Trial: The Records of the International Military Tribunal for the Far East with an Authoritative Commentary and Comprehensive Guide*. Lewiston, NY: Edwin Mellen Press.

Pym, Anthony. (1998a). *Method in Translation History*. Manchester: St. Jerome Publishing.

———. (1998b). "Spanish Tradition," in *Encyclopedia of Translation Studies*, ed. Mona Baker. London and New York: Routledge, pp. 552–63.

———. (1998c). "Okay, So How Are Translation Norms Negotiated?" *Current Issues in Language and Society* 5: 1 & 2, pp. 107–13.

———. (2006). "Introduction: On the Social and Cultural in Translation Studies," in *Sociocultural Aspects of Translation*, ed. Anthony Pym et al. Amsterdam and Philadelphia: John Benjamins, pp. 1–25.

Reel, A. Frank. (1949/1971). *The Case of General Yamashita*. New York: Octagon Books.

Röling, B. V. A., and Antonio Cassese. (1993). *The Tokyo Trials and Beyond: Reflections of a Peacemonger*. Cambridge, MA: Polity Press.

Schafer, Susanne M. (2007, March 9). "Army Translators Hone English at New Fort Jackson School." Associated Press.

Schjoldager, Anne. (1995/2002). "An Exploratory Study of Translational Norms in Simultaneous Interpreting: Methodological Reflections," in *The Interpreting Studies Reader*, ed. Franz Pöchhacker and Miriam Shlesinger. London and New York: Routledge, pp. 301– 11.

Shimada Masakazu. (2000). "Booth no naka no Itami Akira." Interview by Masaomi Kondo and Tomie Watanabe. *Daito Forum* 13, pp. 16–35.

Shimanouchi Tatsuoki. (1973). *Tokyo saiban bengo zatsuroku*. Tokyo: Shimanouchi Tatsuoki.

Shlesinger, Miriam. (1989). "Extending the Theory of Translation to Interpretation: Norms as a Case in Point." *Target* 1:2, pp. 111–15.

———. (1999). "Norms, Strategies and Constraints: How Do We Tell Them Apart?" in *Anovar/Anosar estudios de traducción e interpretación*, ed. A. Álvarez Lugrís and A. Fernández Ocampo, Vol. 1. Vigo: Universidade de Vigo, pp. 65–77.

———. (2001). "Shared Ground in Interpreting Studies Too." *Target* 13:1, pp. 165–68.

Slesnick, Irwin L, and Carole E. (2006). *Kanji and Codes: Learning Japanese for World War II*. Bellingham, WA: Irwin L. and Carole E. Slesnick.

Smith, D. F. (1946, November 25). *Additional Translators, Typists, Equipment and Supplies*. Records of Allied Operational and Occupation Headquarters, World War II (Records Group 331), U.S. National Archives.

Smith, Robert Barr. (1996). "Japanese War Crime Trials." Online at http://www.historynet.com/magazines/world_war_2/3035796.html [consulted March 22, 2010].

Sonnenfeldt, Richard W. (2006). *Witness to Nuremberg*. New York: Arcade Publishing.

Takeda Kayoko. (2009). "War and Interpreters." *Across Languages and Cultures* 10:1, pp. 49–62.

Togo Senso Jiten. (1997 onward). "Masaki Hideki." Online at http://www007.upp.so-net.ne.jp/togo/human/ma/hidekima.html [consulted March 22, 2010].

Torikai Kumiko. (2004). *Rekishi o kaeta goyaku*. Tokyo: Shinchosha.

———. (2009). *Voices of the Invisible Presence*. Amsterdam and Philadelphia: John Benjamins.

Totani Yuma. (2008). *The Tokyo War Crimes Trial: The Pursuit of Justice in the Wake of World War II*. Cambridge, MA: Harvard University Press.

Toury, Gideon. (1978/2000). "The Nature and Role of Norms in Translation," in *The Translation Studies Reader*, ed. Lawrence Venuti. London: Routledge, pp. 198–211.

———. (1995). *Descriptive Translation Studies and Beyond*. Amsterdam and Philadelphia: John Benjamins.

———. (1998). "A Handful of Paragraphs on 'Translation' and 'Norms.'" *Current Issues in Language and Society* 5: 1 & 2, pp. 10–32.

———. (2007). "What Can the Bible Tell Us About Translation in Antiquity?" in *Interpreting Studies and Beyond*, ed. Franz Pöchhacker et al. Copenhagen: Samfundslitteratur Press.

Translator and Interpreter Service. (1946, January 29). *Classification of Linguists*. Records of Allied Operational and Occupation Headquarters, World War II (Records Group 331), U.S. National Archives.

U.S. National Archives. Record Group 238: National Archives Collection of World War II War Crimes Records; Record Group 331: Records of the Allied Operational and Occupation Headquarters, World War II; and Record Group 554: Records of General Headquarters, Far East Command, Supreme Commander Allied Powers, and United Nations Command.

Wadensjö, Cecilia. (1998). *Interpreting as Interaction*. London: Longman.

Walbridge, Vern. (1947, May 8). "Failure to Notify Language Division of Changes in Presentation of Evidence." Records of the Allied Operational and Occupation Headquarters, World War II (Records Group 331), U.S. National Archives.

Watanabe Tomie. (1998). "Tokyo saiban no tsuyaku kenkyu: Tojo Hideki shogen o tsujite." M.A. thesis. Tokyo and Saitama: Daito Bunka University.

Watanabe Tomie. (2000). "Tokyo saiban to monitor no yakuwari."*Daito Forum* 13, pp. 62–70.

Wisconsin Court System. (2002). *Code of Ethics for Court Interpreters*. Online at http://www.wicourts.gov/services/interpreter/ethics.htm [consulted March 22, 2010].

Yamaguchi Reiko. (1984). *Iwamoto Mari ikiru imi*. Tokyo: Shinchosha.

Yamasaki Toyoko. (1983). *Futatsu no Sokoku*. Tokyo: Shincho Bunko.

Yamashiro Masao. (1984). *Tooi taigan: Aru Kibei Nisei no kaiso*. Tokyo: Gorobyusha.

Zarakhovich, Yuri. (2005, October 10). "Signs of the Times." *Time Europe*, pp. 94–95.

INDEX

"f" refers to figure; "t" to table.

Marquis Book Printing Inc.

Québec, Canada
2010